T0109126

Hollywood
in
Heels

Hollywood in Heels

A Small-Town Girl's Adventures in Tinseltown

Charity Gaye Finnestad

Skyhorse Publishing

Copyright © 2013 by Charity Gaye Finnestad
Cover photograph and all interior photographs © Annique Delphine

All Rights Reserved. No part of this book may be reproduced in any manner without the express written consent of the publisher, except in the case of brief excerpts in critical reviews or articles. All inquiries should be addressed to Skyhorse Publishing, 307 West 36th Street, 11th Floor, New York, NY 10018.

Skyhorse Publishing books may be purchased in bulk at special discounts for sales promotion, corporate gifts, fund-raising, or educational purposes. Special editions can also be created to specifications. For details, contact the Special Sales Department, Skyhorse Publishing, 307 West 36th Street, 11th Floor, New York, NY 10018 or info@skyhorsepublishing.com.

www.skyhorsepublishing.com

10 9 8 7 6 5 4 3 2 1

Library of Congress Cataloging-in-Publication Data available on file.

ISBN: 978-1-62636-165-2

Printed in the United States of America

For…
My Magic Man,
Robert Henry Kondrk

My Prince,
Talbot Alexander Kondrk

My Hero,
Peter Lehner

My Soul-Sister Muse,
Annique Delphine

And all the frogs I kissed along the way,
without whom this wouldn't exist.

May you all find your own happily ever after.

AUTHOR'S NOTE

Events in this book may be out of sequence, a few minor characters are composites of more than one person, and conversations were recreated to the best of my ability.

Furthermore, names, dates, and locations have been changed, and a few red herrings were thrown in to confuse would-be sleuths. All of this was done in a concerted effort to protect the guilty. Let's be clear—there are no innocents in this book.

Now that we have that out of the way—everything you are about to read really did happen. As the wise old sage said, "You can't make this shit up!"

CONTENTS

Ass-ettes [**ass**-etz]

noun

1. The bubbles of flesh located at the top of a woman's legs that magically open doors for her and get her where she wants to go in life.
2. Any desirable trait possessed by a female that increases her market value.

Example: "Her ass-ettes took her straight to the top."

UTILIZE YOUR ASS-ETTES

No question about it; I'm a modern-day Alice, and I've fallen down the rabbit hole. There's no other way to explain my current situation. I'm sitting on a stool in a back room of a Hollywood Hills mansion having hot pink feathers glued to my private parts by a complete stranger. Dozens of half-naked women parade around me getting ready for the fashion show we will soon be participating in—if you can call these scraps of lace and fowl I'm wearing fashion. I personally find that to be a large stretch of the imagination.

A tall, silicone-breasted blonde leans over me, pouring her massive naked bosom into my lap. She asks the makeup artist gluing my feathers to apply more bronzer to her areolae. Without pausing, he whips a brush from behind his ear and dusts her big round nipples in powder. That's right—my makeup artist is a guy! A dude! A man! The person disassembling a feather duster and gluing it to my thong and breasts has a cock between his legs. Wait for the real bombshell—I don't think he's gay! I know a straight man when I see one.

Flecks of bronzing powder rain on my bare legs as Big Boobs gives Makeup Dude a thank-you grab to the crotch. He tweaks her nipple. She purrs. I shudder. That's the final straw. I'm officially in shock. Next thing you know, they're going to be making out across my lap. This is most definitely not what I signed up for.

It all sounded so innocent and glamorous last Monday when my supposedly legit modeling agent called me about the job. "It's a lingerie fashion show for an MTV Movie Awards after-party hosted by P. Diddy. Four hundred bucks for two hours' work." I certainly needed the money. I'd run through all my measly savings and had no idea how I was going to pay my rent the next week.

Admittedly, I'd never modeled lingerie before, but how hard could it be? It would be practically the same as wearing a bikini around a pool. As my agent talked on, I imagined a Victoria's Secret-style runway and gorgeous brassieres; maybe I would even get a set of Angel wings. How cool would that be? I was kind of surprised they would pick a model with my less-than-voluminous endowment in the chest area to model lingerie, but according to my agent, they wanted variety. Well, if it was variety they wanted, my skinny legs, pointy hipbones, and bite-sized breasts were happy to oblige.

Even better, I'd heard you normally get to keep the clothes you model. I was certain that would be the case with unmentionables. I was about to acquire a whole new set of panties to replace the ones I'd purchased so long ago that there might still be a pair of Underoos among them. How exciting.

Ha! Silly, naive Charity, fooled again. Undone by her overly optimistic, rose-colored perception of Tinsel Town. There will be no new lacy drawers in my future. No wings. No glamorous moment to brag to my grandkids about when I'm eighty and wrinkly. No sexy brassieres. Zip. Zero. Zilch. Nada. Instead I'm being turned into a freakish Playboy-bunny-meets-Kentucky-Fried-Chicken creature by a man who likes to nipple-tweak strangers (and is dangerously close to mine). They'll probably send me home with a Ziploc baggie of feathers at the end of the night—if I'm lucky, and if the damn things even come off. Otherwise, tomorrow I may be scheduling an emergency appointment with my Russian wax mama, saying, "I have a strange request; do you do feathers?"

I've fallen to a level I didn't even know existed . . . I'm poultry porn!

You might be asking yourself, "How on earth can a girl come to this?" Let alone a good girl who went through twelve years of Christian school and graduated from college *summa cum laude* with degrees in religion and education.

I blame it all on the red carnations.

I grew up in Seattle. Well that's not exactly true. I really grew up in Bellevue, which is essentially the Beverly Hills of Seattle. Everyone there was rich. Everyone, that is, but us. I'm not quite sure how my dad got the deal he did on the fixer-upper house that we never quite fixed up (and which ultimately burned down) on Lakeside Heights. But I'm certain that every neighbor on the block rued the day when the ragamuffin Finnestad clan moved in. They were posh. We were pesky; too loud, too exuberant, too everything. They shopped at Nordstrom, Bloomingdale's, and Saks. We shopped at Value Village, Salvation Army, and Goodwill.

When I couldn't find what I wanted at one of greater Seattle's many thrift stores, I would draw up a design, make a pattern, and my handy mom would whip it together with scrap fabric that my grandma had been hoarding for the end times. I was the luckiest girl alive. I had no idea we were poor. I just thought we were creative. No one else in the entire city looked like me, and I loved it.

At least, I loved it until every horrid Monday morning, when I had to get ready for school. Don't get me wrong; I loved school. I loved everything about it: the books, the assignments, my desk, my teachers, my friends, recess. I even loved the smell of number-two pencils. I was a nerd. A much-loved nerd, but a nerd nonetheless. There was only one glitch in my willing cooperation with the process of educating my young and impressionable mind . . . The fucking uniforms!

Uniforms were, to me, a fate worse than death. The Christian school my parents forced me to attend required them. It was an outrage. I was an artisté, a visionary, a creative. How was a girl to be an original in a conformist uniform? I despised those polyester, navy-blue jumpers with the tiny red stripe of piping, and the white button-down shirt that had to be worn under it. No clothing should ever be made of polyester, and certainly not one you had to wear Monday through Friday for the rest of your elementary school existence.

I knew the instant I saw them sitting in the twenty-five-cent bin at the Value Village check stand that they were my solution; the answer to all my woes. Sure, most people would have just seen a slightly mangled silk flower arrangement—probably made by somebody's grandma at a nursing home, and discarded by the kids the moment she passed away. But I saw something else. I saw what it could be, not what it was. To be precise, I saw two perfectly round, fire-engine red, plastic-stemmed, fluffy bunches of individuality.

I begged my mom to let me buy them. I know it sounds crazy, but twenty-five cents was a lot to us back then. My mom wasn't about to let me waste it on a scrappy former Christmas arrangement that hadn't even been nice enough for the original owner to keep. Half the flowers in it were missing their petals, and the ones that weren't had a slightly moldy smell to them. It took some formidable skills of persuasion and a few fake tears, but ultimately I convinced her that I could not live without those big red carnations gracing the center of that raggedy bouquet. Worn down, my mom conceded. Handing me a shiny silver quarter, she sealed my fate.

That was a Saturday.

I spent all weekend imagining just what I would do with those juicy red carnations. Come Monday morning, I was ready. I carefully pulled my hair into two of the highest ponytails ever to grace Seattle's Puget Sound. I plucked the flowers from the arrangement and sprayed Bonnie Bell perfume on them to cover the mildew odor. Then carefully, so as not to pull any hairs loose, I poked the green plastic stems of my red beacons of individuality into my ponytails. It was perfect. I was perfect. I was 100 percent me.

Sure, I still had to wear the silly uniform, but it no longer bothered me. It was clear then that no other attire would showcase the radiant red of my gorgeous fake flowers like those ugly polyester contraptions. Why, I even grew to appreciate the uniforms. Without them, everyone could have been individual; unique in their own right. With them, I was the only one who somehow figured out how to stand apart. Everybody needs a little wind beneath their wings, and my navy-blue jumper was just what my floral puffs of personality needed to soar.

The red carnations were just the beginning of my addiction to a little drug called creativity. Soon I was experimenting with scarves around my neck, chopsticks in my hair, and leg warmers around my ankles. You know what they say about drugs; there is no going back once you start. I was never going back, or so I thought.

Three years later, tragedy struck my eccentric family. A car accident on a holiday vacation killed our littlest member: my beautiful sister, Melody Joy. Fleeing the scene of the memories and starting fresh in a new town was the only way my parents could cope. Unfortunately for me, the place they chose for that new beginning was a tourist trap called Sisters, smack in the middle of Oregon—a town so small that it didn't even have a traffic light.

I've come to the conclusion that the size of a town's population is in direct proportion to the diversity of the town's mindset. Am I calling small towns small-minded? Yes! I most certainly am. Conformity is the name of the game, and fitting in is the only hope you have of not suffering total isolation and loneliness. It's not like you had the option of whom to befriend. There were two groups: the cool kids who wore Lacoste polo shirts and had lived in that Podunk town their whole lives, and you.

Hey, I thought I was cool (or at the very least interesting) when I arrived in Sisters. I was in my mauve princess prom dress pinned with safety pins over stirrup pants, accompanied by a pair of high black boots (to hide the fact that my pants were highwaters) phase. How can stirrup pants be highwaters, you might ask? Simple—I cut the stirrups and added a couple of inches of white elastic to the bottom to enable them to stretch enough to cover my ridiculously long legs. Let's face it. There wasn't a special department for tall, skinny chicks at Kmart. All my pants were flood-proof. Unfortunately, white elastic does not do much for black stirrup pants. That's where the boots came in. Genius. A better solution didn't exist. Style *and* practicality; I looked great!

Unfortunately, the inhabitants of Central Oregon failed to see the beauty of my creativity. They just thought I was weird. Sure, I had an equally weird family that I could hang out with, but the more time I spent with them, the more I was reminded that my favorite member was gone, and I would never get to see her laughing eyes again. It was the darkest, loneliest time of my life. I couldn't bring my sister back, and I couldn't go home to Seattle where there were people who loved me in spite of all my idiosyncrasies.

Fuck! The people in Sisters didn't even know Melody had ever lived. What did they care if my heart was shred to pieces from missing her, and from their rejection of me? They were too busy being cool, and having someone to contrast themselves with made them feel even cooler.

I could only hold out for so long. A year after moving there, I surrendered.

Yes, I was an artisté, but I was also a person—a deeply social person who needed friends and love. I decided that if they didn't love me as I was, I would become whatever I needed to be in order to be loved. The red carnations went in a box, and normal Charity was born.

Never one to do things halfway, I took normal to a level that few people would dream to go. I took good, small-town Christian girl to unprecedented heights. I started out by donating the mauve princess prom dress to a Goodwill Store. Maybe some other original would find it and appreciate it for all its greatness. I needed to find myself some knock-off Lacoste polo shirts. Unfortunately, there were no garment districts in Central Oregon with street vendors bartering fake Lacoste polo shirts on the corner, so I was forced to buy the Kmart polo with a tiny puppy on it instead of the essential crocodile. It didn't fool anyone, but at least I didn't stand out as horribly in photos from a distance.

Next, I became the most active member of the Assembly of God Youth Group on this side of the Rio Grande. I baked cookies, organized car washes, taught Sunday school, worked at summer camp, and even lead worship services. Okay, so maybe I had a passion for super-short shorts that upset my youth pastor, and every once in a while I would start quoting *The Art of War*, Pablo Neruda, or Victor Hugo (evidencing my complete nerdiness). But aside from those minor aberrations, I was doing a pretty good job of faking normal.

Before I knew it, I was graduating high school two years early at the great age of sixteen. That's what happens when your creativity is in a closet and discipline is your only master. I blinked, and I was twenty years old, standing on a podium at Eugene Bible College being draped in *summa cum laude* tassels. As I looked out over the sea of black gowns, I couldn't stop thinking, "How did I get here?" I don't even remember thinking about what I wanted to study, let alone learning anything.

During that same period of time, I married my high school boyfriend. Don't act shocked. Every small-town Christian girl knew that eighteen was a perfectly acceptable age to get married. After all, you weren't supposed to have sex unless you were married, and I really wanted to have sex. Yes, it's true; this poultry porn star was a virgin on her wedding night. No joke! There ought to be a law against marrying your high school boyfriend. Of course it didn't work! We were kids who had no bloody clue who we were. But did I learn? Oh no. I just figured I'd done it wrong the first time, so I had better try again. If God thought marrying once was good, then twice must be better—so I did it again at age twenty-four. That's right—still living in a small town, married twice to two wrong guys, and not even a quarter of a century old!

I was trying to master normal.

The real Charity was tucked away in a shoebox with two puffy red carnations. This Charity was the one they wanted. Truthfully, I didn't like her very much. In fact, I think if I'd had any more normal in my life, I would have died an abnormal death just to escape all of the normalcy. I'd lost myself completely, and I was miserable.

Since childhood, there was one thing in life that had deeply disturbed me to the core: birds in cages. Every time I saw one of those helpless little creatures confined to those cramped quarters, I experienced a feeling of total panic.

Everything about the anatomy of a bird was made to fly. Its light skeletal structure, its wings, its feathers—all were beautifully engineered by nature for the express purpose of flight. It wasn't that birds wanted to fly. It wasn't that they dreamt of flying. It was that they were created to fly. It was their destiny, their nature, their right. A bird in a cage was a crime against that bird's very nature.

I woke up one cold February morning—three years into my second marriage, and still in Oregon—to the nightmarish realization that I was a bird in a cage! The worst part was, I was also the jerk who had constructed the cage and trapped myself in it. Never mind that my cage was an unhappy marriage that I had entered too young, and a beautiful three-bedroom house on the river in old-town Bend, Oregon. It was still a cage, and I was still supposed to be flying—not bumping around in that tiny, self-imposed, religion-induced, mind-bogglingly limiting space.

I was miserable. I hadn't thought for myself or done a single creative thing in years—except for my closet writing. What's more, that would be the way I would feel for the rest of my life unless I was willing to take a colossal risk and escape the cage to learn to do what my very DNA demanded I should do.

Fly!

I was terrified. But after that cold, February-morning realization, it wasn't really a choice. I knew that if I didn't leave, I was in real danger of my spirit dying. My body might linger, but my spirit, the thing that gave life its spark and purpose, would be gone. I'd seen it happen before; people who were walking around going through the motions, but no longer alive. I couldn't let that happen to me. The question was no longer *if* I would leave the cage. The question was: Would I still know how to fly once I did? Also, there was that tiny little detail of where on earth would

I go? I didn't belong anywhere. I certainly didn't belong in Oregon. I hadn't belonged there since the day I'd pulled into town in my mauve prom dress. It didn't take a genius to figure out that the place was toxic for someone like me.

I needed a big city. In fact, I needed a very specific big city.

Since my elementary school days spent trudging through drippy, grey Seattle in my galoshes and raincoat, I'd fantasized about moving to Los Angeles. From my soggy state, I imagined living in a place where the sun shone every day, where palm trees swayed in the breeze, and where movie stars strolled through streets in evening gowns and tiaras nightly. I cut out hundreds of pictures of palm trees and sandy beaches from travel magazines and glued them to my bedroom window. Never mind that some weren't even photos of Los Angeles, but beaches in Hawaii, Fiji, and Thailand. The point was that they were what Tinsel Town embodied to me.

With my all-consuming love for La La Land, you would think that I would have packed my bags and hit Interstate 5 for my own personal paradise the minute I graduated high school. But no, I was a chicken. Like the schoolgirl who watched her crush from a distance—more content to live in her fantasy that he secretly yearned for her too, than to approach him and risk actual rejection—I worshipped from afar. I comforted myself with a blanket of grown-up cynicism. Everyone dreamt of going to Hollywood and becoming a big shot. Nobody actually achieved it. They're all really miserable there anyway. Fame sucked, there was no privacy. It was too big of a city; who wanted to deal with the crazy traffic? The people were all shallow. A small, humble life was more rewarding than a bullshit celebrity life. I could have had it if I wanted it, but I didn't really want it. I wanted to live in a boring, sleepy, one-horse ski town. I wasn't watching Hollywood gossip shows and dreaming of being part of the inside club. I was cooler than them right there in my pink sweats, tee-shirt, and slippers, sitting in front of my TV eating potato chips and drinking Corona. On and on the self-denial went. It was easier to piously pretend I didn't care (while sneaking sideways glances at the field) than to admit that I desperately wanted to play. At least that way there was no chance of making a fool of myself by going for it and failing. Besides, I had the best excuse of all; love and self-sacrifice. So there I sat in Central Oregon, rotting away from the inside out on unfulfilled ambitions of greatness.

The morning I woke up and saw myself as a bird in a cage, it was clear that this way of life had to end! I realized that if I was ever going to take the plunge and tackle the City of Angels, I had to do it right away. I couldn't wait any longer. Time was flying, and I wasn't getting any younger. As it was, everyone else was going to have a massive head start on me. I made a plan. I gave myself two months to wrap up my life in Oregon and leave.

Exactly two months from the day I made that decision (April 15, 2002), I pulled into Tinsel Town. I arrived with the standard baggage of those who find themselves drawn to this gorgeous mirage in the desert: a pocket full of dreams, an anorexic bank account, and a delusional belief in my own self-worth in this illustrious city. I'd secretly dreamed of being a writer my whole life. Every night since my sister had died, unbeknownst to anyone, I poured out my heart in journals. I wrote the mundane details of my existence; I wrote poetry and short stories. I wrote ideas for scripts. I wrote nonsense. I just wrote. Like my heroes Anaïs Nin, Ayn Rand, Victor Hugo, and Ernest Hemingway, I expressed my deepest secrets, desires, and beliefs with words on paper.

I had no idea how I was going to transform those private written words into a public forum and profession. I had no idea what specific form they would take when I tried: books, screenplays, or poetry. But I was convinced that in LA, it would all come together and be crystal clear. I'd seen *Biography*, *Before They Were Stars*, and *Making of a Star*. I knew all the tastemakers in LA were prowling the streets, grocery stores, and Coffee Beans looking for those individuals that had the "it factor," ready to turn them into an overnight sensation. I was pretty sure I had an extra dose of "it-ness," and that I would no doubt be discovered the minute

I pulled into town. Boy was it a shock when I'd been in LA for two weeks, and no one had managed to "discover" me yet. They had better get a move on; I only had enough savings to survive for approximately sixty days. They had already wasted fourteen of them.

By day fifty, I was panicked. Clearly this city didn't work the way it did in the movies and TV shows I'd seen. Talk about false advertising. Obviously I was going to have to "discover" my destiny and direction on my own, instead of relying on those lackadaisical tastemakers to do their job. That was fine; I was quite confident that with a little bit of time and hard work I could do it, but therein lay the problem. I wasn't afraid of hard work, but time? That was another issue. Last time I checked, it took money to keep a roof over your head and food in your mouth. My money was going to be gone in ten days' time.

That was my worried frame of my mind as I sat in Fred Segal's café, studying the numbers in my bankbook and hoping they would magically change. Fred Segal's was to me what Tiffany's was to Holly Golightly; my safe place in the mad, crazy world in which I'd found myself. Sure, like Holly, I couldn't afford a single thing in the joint except the over-priced tea I clutched in my hands and nursed as slowly as I could in hopes of occupying the real estate at my table as long as possible. But I still loved the feel of the place and dreamed of a day when I could walk in and buy anything I wanted.

Out of nowhere, I was yanked from my desperate musings by a well-dressed woman extending a business card toward me.

"I don't know if you have representation already, but if not, I'd love to have you come by the agency and chat."

"Representation?"

"You are a model, aren't you?"

Eureka! My ridiculous height and chopstick legs were good for some-thing! Here was the solution to all my problems. I hadn't even considered modeling. Sure, I'd done a bit growing up, but I'd never been particularly good at it. I had a tendency to grin whenever a camera was pointed at me, and I was fully aware that once you hit twenty in modeling years, you were over-the-hill and going down the other side. I was twenty-eight, which made me a dinosaur. So of course I replied, "Absolutely. And no, I don't have representation in LA yet."

"Well, come in Monday at noon and bring your book."

Yikes. I'd forgotten that pesky part of the equation. Your book is the primary tool every model needs to get work. A good book can take you a long way. Mine was a horrid conglomeration of knitting catalogue photos, bridal magazine shots, and small-town store ads. I was never going to get anywhere with it in LA. Not to mention that the cheesy portfolio happened to be located in a storage box in the basement of my mom's home in Oregon.

"I'll be there."

A crisis like that called for creative thinking, and creative I was. With the help of my starving photo assistant next-door neighbor and a little Photoshop magic, we managed to whip together a fake book that looked like I'd worked for European brands whose ads no one here in the States would recognize. It was genius.

There were only eight photos in my "book," but it was enough to get me in the door. That, and the fact that I lied about my age. I was terrified about that one. Monday afternoon when I said, "Twenty-three," I expected her jaw to drop and for her to point at me and yell, "Liar!" like in *The Princess Bride*.

Instead she responded, "You don't look a day over nineteen. I'll sell you as nineteen."

A woman after my own heart.

An hour after I arrived at the agency, I was sent to my first casting by my brand-spanking-new rep: a big lingerie fashion show for P. Diddy's MTV Movie Awards after-party.

I booked the job. My luck had changed!

"Okay sugar, you're up."

Jolted out of my memories, I look at Makeup Dude, who's pointing me toward a line of lingerie-clad girls marching onto a brightly lit stage. Glancing down at myself I see a plethora of skin and a few carefully placed feathers.

"Wait, what? Are you sure this is the right number of feathers?"

Laughing, he yanks two of the feathers off my butt. "You're right. Now you're good." Smacking my ass, he nods toward the line. "Get out there. You're the fine-feathered finale of the show. Make me proud." Shaking like a leaf, I teeter on four-inch hooker shoes toward the line. Just as I reach the end, Big Boobs steps out onto the stage to a rousing round of applause.

Standing backstage—with nerves flooding my stomach and urging me to run for my life—I attempt to bolster my resolve. I made a commitment to do this, I can't walk out now. I need the money. I need the agent. Sure, this isn't exactly how I imagined making my mark on Tinsel Town, but until I discover my highly elusive destiny, a girl's gotta do what a girl's gotta do to survive. If utilizing my ass-ettes will get me to a place where I can finally sport my carnations and reveal my real assets, then I don't see any way around it. Besides, that room out there must be loaded with tastemakers. Surely one of them will have the foresight to see my dazzling "it-ness" through the haze of pink feathers.

Hey, I hadn't even thought of that. I just needed to be in the right place at the right time. Maybe this is it. Maybe I've finally arrived. This could be the first day of the rest of my life.

Stop the presses! Charity Gaye Finnestad is about to be discovered!

With that thought pumping through my veins like cocaine, I shake a tail feather onto the stage and into my glorious future.

Day Flaking [dā **flāk**-ing]
verb
1. The common Hollywood practice of canceling a meeting with
   a friend or associate at the last second because you speculate
   that you might garner more profit from meeting with someone
   else or taking a nap.

Note: In day flaking, the *flaked on* frequently is not notified that the *flakee* will not show up. Thus the Coffee Beans and Tea Leafs of Tinsel Town are full of victims who stare at the door each time it opens, only to drop their head in dismay when they do not recognize the entrant.

Fact: New York has day trading. Los Angeles has day flaking.

THE ORIGINAL GERMAN

The German, my new best friend, wriggles the key in the lock and pushes the front door open. She turns on the lights and heads for the kitchen. I follow her inside. Across the cream-carpeted living room I see my destination: a futon couch, my home for the past three nights.

Drawing on my inner balance, I gingerly navigate the minefield separating me from the couch. Up, down, twist, turn, and twist again. I deftly place my heel-clad feet between the hundreds of pellets littering the floor, ever so careful not to mash any into the carpet. Suddenly I feel moisture oozing between my toes. Oh, crap! I didn't see that pee puddle. I swear, I'm going to kill those bunnies.

Bunnies—that's correct, as in rabbits. The German's roommate—Her Royal Low-ness, the unacknowledged offspring of a Playboy bunny and an aging TV star—has recently acquired two rabbits for pets. Unfortunately, she's also acquired the crazy idea that putting rabbits in a cage hinders their emotional freedom and development. Wanting her bunnies to grow up to be fully functioning members of rabbit society, she's arbitrarily decided to allow them free reign of her (and the German's) pad. Since bunnies have no concept of using toilets, the place looks like a case of cocoa puffs exploded and smells like a rancid cat litter box. Like most of us who enjoy walking through our homes without maneuvering around bunny piss and shit, the German is not happy about it, but she has given up on the battle.

Slowed down, but not defeated by the unexpected pee puddle, I'm just about to reach my home, the couch, when I hear the German scream from the kitchen.

"Bitch! I swear to God, I'm going to pee in her wheat grass juice!"

The German storms into the living room waving a piece of pastel-pink paper in the air like a matador does his cape.

"What happened? Whose wheat grass juice?"

I watch in horror as the German marches toward me, squishing pile after pile of poo into the carpet. She doesn't even notice that remnants are sticking to the bottom of her once-perfect Louis Vuittons.

Upon reaching me, my usually calm friend shoves the pink stationery in my face. Looking down, I see an evil message camouflaged in big girlie handwriting.

Dear German,

I've given our situation a lot of thought, and karma is very important. If your friend is going to be staying with us, I want to help her maintain the balance in her karma account. To do that, she is going to need to pay rent. I will be expecting an $800 check by the end of the week for her share of this month. I also need an $800 deposit. Just in case she accidentally does any damage to the apartment.

Namaste.

Her Royal Low-ness

My jaw drops. Is this girl for real? Damage to the apartment? What could I possibly do to trash the place worse than her bunnies already have? Carve my name into the walls? Squat and take a dump on the carpet? Burn swastikas into the countertops? Besides, if I could bloody well afford sixteen hundred dollars for rent and a deposit on a place, I sure as hell wouldn't be sleeping on a tiny couch in a den full of rabbit dung! I crumple the pink paper into a ball and burst into tears.

"Oh no you don't!" The German grabs the ball of paper and sends it soaring across the land of poo.

"This is not something to cry about, this is something to get pissed about!"

"But I don't have anywhere to go," I wail.

Throwing her arms around me, the German assures me, "We'll figure this out."

It's amazing how much you can come to rely on someone you've only known for two weeks.

It was exactly fifteen days ago, on my first job as an extra, that I met her. My modeling agent had booked the job for me, and I didn't have a clue what I was doing.

They told me it was a cakewalk: "Call time is at six a.m. Be there in sexy party clothes, and bring a backup outfit in case they don't like the one you're wearing. Just think it's like going to a party, but you get paid to do it. Enjoy."

Let me tell you, getting ready at five a.m. in nightclub attire was no picnic. There was a reason you drank when you went out—you needed to take the self-consciousness out of your outfit and make the four-inch heels bearable. Without the booze, both were unnatural. Unfortunately, when I got to the set, the wardrobe person chose my highest heels and skimpiest "I don't really want to have to wear this" backup outfit. I had no choice but to change.

Looking almost naked and feeling terribly self-conscious, I was herded into a room and told to wait with the two hundred other extras booked for the job. Two hours later, we were still waiting. Everyone else had something to entertain themselves with: books, games, knitting projects. I had nothing. Clearly my genius agent had forgotten to warn me to bring something "to do" to "the party." Restless, I sat and stared at the strange assortment of characters around me. I could honestly say that, in my whole life, I'd never seen so many weirdos in one room. Where were the glamorous movie star types?

A creepy ax murderer-like guy kept giving me a "hey baby" once-over and licking his lips. My skin crawled. The hundredth time his tongue came out, I jumped from my seat and bolted for the bathroom. I couldn't take it anymore. When I returned, I snuck to another part of the room, hoping he wouldn't see me. Much to my dismay, I realized that my new seating companion, a totally harmless-looking fellow, was a compulsive nose picker. Gross! Wasn't there anywhere I could go that was free of freaks? I moved again. This time, I sat next to two girls. That should have been safe. Ten minutes after I took my seat, the Hippy Chick who was sitting across from me pulled a plastic bag of brownies from her purse and offered me one. Now that was more like it! Starving, I accepted one and thanked her. Maybe there was a person I could befriend. As I went to put the brownie in my mouth, though, she dropped the bomb.

"I hope you like them. I made them special with breast milk."

Gagging, I yanked the brownie out of my mouth and ran for the bathroom. Again!

This time, I made sure to find a spot all by myself when I came out. Wedged between the vending machines and the bathroom hall, I sat on a cold metal folding chair losing my patience. What was taking so long? Wasn't shooting expensive? Weren't they on a budget? Didn't they need to get us out there soon? Maybe I needed to go back to that check-in booth and make sure I was in the right place. There must have been some mistake. Surely I didn't belong here with all these freaks. I was an original, not a freak.

Suddenly I was yanked from my musings by a six-foot Helmut Newton-esque model with the kind of beauty that makes blind men do double-takes. She slid into the seat next to me and crossed her ridiculously long legs.

"First time?" she said.

"Is it that obvious?" I asked, wondering if I had a sign on my forehead that declared me a greenhorn.

"Well, you didn't bring anything to do, and you don't look wasted enough to have come from last night's party like I did."

Seriously? I was in awe.

"You mean you came straight from partying to here?"

"Powering through made more sense than getting up at five. Besides, I don't have an internal clock."

And that's how the most amazing and interesting person I'd ever known blasted into my life, and how I first learned about her bizarre sleep habits. She was a force of nature. A goddess. A dork. A dreamer. A wild child. A muse. A model. A photographer. An inspiration. A German. Soon to become *my* German.

Neither the German nor I had anything to do, and clearly they were never going to have us work, so we started talking. By eleven a.m., we were up-to-date on each other's childhoods, first kisses, first sex, first loves, first heartbreaks, first jobs, last jobs, first moments in LA, and rapidly approaching present day. I can talk a lot. The German can talk more. I was pretty sure that by the end of the day, neither one of us would have a single secret left.

At eleven-thirty, they finally put us to work, if you can call it that. We were supposed to dance to nonexistent music at a pretend nightclub while the stars of the show said their lines. The director would blast five seconds of "Wild Thing" by Tone Loc to put us in the right mindset, then they would cut the music and yell, "Tape." We were to keep dancing in silence to an inner loop of "I get paid to do the Wild Thang . . ." There's nothing like watching a bunch of strangers bumping and grinding to silence. What was even weirder was how all of the girls were acting like wannabe strippers at an audition, busting out their naughtiest pole dance moves in the hopes of getting into the background of a shot.

Except for the German. She just wanted to get paid and go home and sleep off her hangover. But if she had to be there and dance to nothingness with a bunch of freaks, she was damn well going to have a fun time doing it. She busted out her funky chicken, her moonwalk, and her robot. She did everything she could to stay out of the shot behind the masses while she entertained me with a host of dance moves that would make grown men weep—with laughter, that is.

I'm pretty sure it was her goal to get me busted for laughing out loud, and then she would play innocent. Like my little brothers used to do in church. My kidneys hurt from struggling to hold in the laughter. When she flung one arm in the air John Tavolta-style, and did a Michael Jackson crotch grab with the other, it was all I could do not to pee my pants (I mean, miniskirt). Tears made my nightclub makeup smear across my face. Several times we got the evil eye from one of the sexy pole dancers who felt we were not imbuing the shoot with the gravitas it deserved. They were right. We thought it was a joke. Who could take themselves seriously doing this?

The German and I didn't mind being part of the joke. We loved it. We were high on life. Why wouldn't we be? On that dirty, cheesy set, doing silly ridiculous things, we had discovered something wonderful and profound. Something we had both been missing on our lonely sojourns through LA. We had found a soulmate. A sister spirit. A girl who ate from the same tree of red carnations. A fellow original.

When we broke for lunch, the German and I were ecstatic. Today was turning out to be the best day ever.

Practically tied to the hip, we approached a long line leading to a lunch cart laden with hot cooked meals and an ice cream sundae bar. The smells had me salivating. This was a far cry from the 99 Cent Store noodles I'd been living on for the past few weeks. I couldn't wait to get my hands on one of those juicy burgers. From now on, I was going to do every extra job that came my way. So what if you had to be surrounded by a few freaks? This was a great gig! They fed you burgers and paid you to make a best friend. This was the happiest I'd been since I arrived in town. Maybe I was going to find my niche in the world after all.

After what seemed like an eternity, the German and I finally reached the front of the line. Just as I reached for a plate, I was stopped by a six-foot-seven, ugly-as-sin, three-hundred-pound security guard asking for my union card. What union card? I'd no clue what he was talking about. The German pulled a laminated card out of her cleavage and flashed it at him.

"She left hers inside." She covered for me, but the Giant wasn't having it.

"You're not union, you eat over there." He pointed to a sad-looking, picked-over table of week-old sandwiches. He was thrilled to be putting me in my place. I wanted to cry.

That's when I first learned the hierarchy of Hollywood sets.

Turns out, all extras were not created equal. There were actually classes of extras, and I, the green newbie in town, was of the lower-class variety. I was non-union, which meant that they paid me fifty-four dollars a day to do what the German made one hundred and fifteen to do. I wasn't even worth 50 percent of her. Turns out I wasn't even worth 50 percent of Ax Murderer Dude, the Booger Picking Guy, or Breast Milk Brownie Lady. I was, in fact, the lowliest person on set, and now that lunch had come, everyone knew it. My badge of non-union shame was blazoned across my chest for everyone to see.

The German explained it all as she slid her plate with a burger and a heap of fries across the table to me.

"It's all yours. Hope you like the works, 'cause I put it all on."

Picking mold off the crusts of my sandwich, I pushed her burger back.

"Thank you, but I can't take your food."

My new friend refused to listen. Shoving her plate at me, she yanked the moldy sandwich out of my hand and tossed it across the room toward a trashcan. It missed. I gaped. She didn't notice.

"You're not. I got it for you. I saw you salivating over the burgers. All I wanted was this." She plunged her spoon into her hot fudge sundae and inhaled a bite. "I'm on an all-ice cream diet. I have a big shoot next week." That was when I first learned about the German's bizarre eating habits.

Not one to look a gift burger in the mouth, I picked up the works and raised it toward my starved face.

"You mean to tell me you are making more than twice as much as me for the same job?"

"Yep. That's Hollywood."

"That's bullshit."

"We need to get you in the union."

I'm pretty sure that was the exact moment I became the German's new pet project.

As if attempting to get me a union card wasn't enough, the German decided she was going to overhaul my entire existence. I'd been living in a rent-by-the-week excuse for a hotel, and I was running out of money fast. The seedy dive not only posed as a set for a murder scene you might see on the late-night news, it also had the audacity to charge obscene amounts of money for providing a cockroach-infested roof over your head. I hadn't been able to move out because I was caught in a catch-22. To find a better place, I would need to come up with enough savings to have a deposit and first and last month's rent, but because the hellhole charged so much, I couldn't save a single dime—even when I managed to make one. So there I'd sat, spinning my wheels and praying for a miracle.

The German was my miracle.

Within two weeks of befriending me and taking me under her wing, she decided I would move out of the hotel and onto her couch. She figured that by the end of one month, I would have been able to save enough money to get my own piece of the Southern California dream, or at least a closet of it.

Sure, her place wouldn't have been my first choice, given the crazy roommate with the shitting bunnies, but beggars can't be choosers, and she did have a point. Staying where I was, I was only going to end up broke and living in the Little Pip (my beat-up Honda Civic) before the month's end. A poop-surrounded couch seemed safer than the front seat of a car for a cute single girl to be sleeping on in the big bad city. Besides, I didn't have a lot of options. It wasn't as if the tastemakers were beating down my door to accost me with opportunities and wealth.

And that's how I found myself living with my new best friend.

I burst into a fresh round of tears as I look at the crumpled pink paper lying across the room and realize it's all about to come to an end. Why did my sister-soulmate have to come with a crazy roommate? And how on earth did Her Royal Low-ness figure that my two-by-six-foot space of couch, borrowed for only eight hours a night, is equivalent to half of her one thousand-square-foot suite with adjoining bathroom? But there wasn't much I could say or do to argue with her. This was half her place; not mine at all. In fact, I didn't have a single inch in the world to call my own right now. It was too gruesome for words.

"Look, you're not going anywhere!" the German insists.

"I have an idea. Forget the couch. You'll stay in my room. I'd bloody like to see the bitch try to charge you rent for half of my bed. I'll charge her for all the guys she brings home to screw every night. I'll give them an hourly rate."

I look at her. She's totally serious. My tears turn to laughter as I imagine the German standing at the door, sexy as hell in a pair of heels, handing out accommodation bills to every bemused Tom, Dick, and Harry Her Royal Low-ness sleeps with as they sneak out in the middle of the night. I can't help myself.

"You'll be rich in two months' time!"

The German busts into laughter. There we sit, amidst the shit, laughing like loons.

I may be down, but apparently as long as I've got the German in my life, I will never really be out. She won't have it! Even if it means sharing her slice of the American/German pie and sleeping with my scrawny body squashed up against hers in a twin bed for the next three weeks. She'll do it. A little self-sacrifice doesn't faze her. She's in for the long haul.

It's official. After three months of surface encounters, aborted attempts at friendships with strangers, and nights of crying myself to sleep with loneliness, I'm no longer by myself in Tinsel Town. I have my first real friend—the German. The one, the only, and a true original!

Tinsel Talk [**tin**(t)-səl tok]

noun

1. A modern language spoken throughout Tinsel Town that employs common English vernacular, yet somehow manages to endow it with a whole new contradictory meaning.

Common Phrases Translated:

Common English Phrase:

"Absolutely! Next week."

Tinsel Talk Translation:

"Sure it was great meeting you, and we shared a moment, but we'll probably never see each other again. Should we happen to run into each other at some future event, we'll give each other air kisses and pretend nothing meaningful ever passed between us."

Common English Phrase:

"Let's have a meeting and discuss your projects."

Tinsel Talk Translation:

"I want to fuck your brains out, so I'm trying to think of a last-ditch way to see you again, since it's clear you are not the least bit interested in me."

THE PERFECT POLICE

Prepping like soldiers going into combat for our first attempt at Operation Legs, the German and I don our shortest skirts and highest heels. My skirt is so short that I'm afraid even breathing will flash my lace boxer shorts. The German, fearless as ever, is going commando. Grabbing a comb, a can of super-hold hairspray, and a handful of hair, we begin the process of teasing our hair into towering beehives. We don't stop until our mops protrude from our heads as massive four-inch bouffants. When we're finished, we each stand at a towering six-feet-four-inches tall. We're as ready as we are ever going to be.

We approach the club, our target destination, and see a line three times the normal length snaking around the building, and a pile of paparazzi standing in front. Clearly an A-List celebrity is inside, and the Perfect Police are going to be even more dastardly than usual. I clutch the German's hand as we march past the end of the line in a beeline for the front. My heart is beating out of my chest as we pass all the people we used to wait with. They look at us in disgust. I hear one mumble, "Who the fuck do they think they are?" I'm asking myself the same question. I feel like a foreigner approaching customs, hoping my thirty-six-inch-long passports have the correct stamps to allow me entry into the land of dreams. We get closer and I feel like turning and running to the back and pretending this never happened. Maybe they won't notice that we were so presumptuous. Maybe if we go back, everything will be okay.

The German doesn't slow down. Since my hand is clutched in hers, neither do I. I know she's just as nervous, because her palms are sweating, but clearly she's not turning back. The German on a mission is an unstoppable force. I can hear her pep talk from earlier that day ringing in my ears.

"Either we belong on the inside, or we don't. If we belong in there, then why the fuck are we always standing out in the cold, hoping for entrance? We're going for it, Charity. Our time has come."

We get to the front and stop cold in our tracks. It's the Dragon Lady, the most ferocious promoter in town, a legend of cutthroat party perfection. This woman has a chip on her shoulder the size of Gibraltar. She lives for chewing up arrogant little line-crashers and sending them home in humiliation, vowing revenge. It's just our luck that she would be the gatekeeper on the one night we decide to be bold. What was I thinking, letting the German talk me into this?

Settling into a new city is always a daunting task, but settling into Los Angeles is a feat like no other. Never in my life have I seen a city where the length of one's legs, the size of one's breasts, or the whiteness of one's smile play such a crucial role in social viability. Let's face it—these things can get you far anywhere, but in LA, they're actually residency requirements. I'm pretty convinced there's a secret society of Perfect Police who keep the less physically blessed from entering city limits. It's not nice, but it's true.

The German and I have often speculated about their weekly meetings. We imagine them lounging in a cabana by a pool, sipping martinis and ruthlessly inspecting stacks of photos of the newly transplanted Los Angelinos. Three stacks of photos sit in front of them. The first is the acceptable—consisting of models, cheerleaders, football captains, and the most beautiful people from small towns all across the globe. This group will be welcomed slowly; brought into the fold one social event at a time. Allowed to join the insiders' club after a period of painful initiation guaranteed to make them feel small and aware of how precarious their positions are. They will be allowed to stay only as long as they maintain their physical perfection.

The next stack is the could-be-acceptable-with-a-little-work group. They'd be considered perfectly attractive anywhere else in the world, but to meet LA standards, they need to lose a few pounds, get a nose job, or consult a stylist. These ones will be made to feel so bad that they will straighten up, starve themselves, pump weights, or get plastic surgery until they can fit into the acceptable category. Those who do not move categories in six months will be driven into the third and final category: the totally unacceptable.

The totally unacceptable, unless they're incredibly rich or related to someone famous, do not stand a chance. They're the target pile. Systematically, they will be driven out of town until all trace of their existence is expelled. The method: social isolation. They will not be allowed into any of the desirable nightclubs, bars, restaurants, parties, or events. They will be made to feel less worthy, less valuable, and unloved. Soon they will be so unhappy and isolated that they will do exactly what they're supposed to do—pack their bags and leave.

You think we jest? Clearly you have not spent time in LA and met the elite group of social police, otherwise known as promoters.

What is a promoter, you ask? How do they hold such supreme power? I'll tell you! The promoter is a predatory animal who considers it a sacred duty to fill the hottest nightclubs, restaurants, and bars with celebrities, the wealthy, and the most perfect specimens of human form. Really good promoters even have the balls to throw in the occasional punk rebel for amusement and variety. To be a promoter, there are two primary requirements: a heart as cold as ice, and the total inability to smile. Note please: the occasional lifting of the corners of one's mouth to show a flash of teeth to a celebrity does not disqualify you; we all know this is not a real smile.

It's twisted, but that's the way it works at the hot clubs of the moment in the City of Angels, and mind you, I do mean the moment! The life span of a LA hot spot is generally shorter than the life span of the common housefly. The phrase, "Oh, that was so five minutes ago," originated in Hollywood and should be interpreted quite literally. Maybe it's a reflection of the entire community's ADD that they can't even commit to a nightclub for six months.

In this climate of superficial values where the promoters have the power of demigods, the German and I have decided to try a bold and daring experiment. For two months now, we've had the great fortune of attending the coolest clubs and parties in town, but not quite the way we'd expected.

It started when the German's modeling agent told us, "Hey girls, I've put you on the list for a magazine launch party. Go represent." We went to the party, super excited for VIP treatment, but quickly found out that being on the list in Hollywood means nothing. We stood in a long line ornamenting the sidewalk with dozens of other partygoers who also had the audacity to think they might be allowed in just because they were on the list. We soon learned that the rules of this game aren't that simple.

In normal lines, the only hurdle one faces is personal patience and willingness to wait for the line to progress until one reaches the front. It is a fairly straightforward practice learned in preschool along with the vitally important lesson of "no cutting!" But these lines are a whole different animal, and a decidedly less democratic one. These are the lines of dictators, class systems, queens, kings, pawns, and jokers—where, despite the fact that you stood for hours waiting your turn, others can saunter right past you to be greeted with air kisses and welcomed in while you are kept out in the cold.

This is not the United States of America. This is Hollywood.

In this medieval theater of life, the German and I have proven to be the lucky ones who always seem to eventually get in. But it has not been easy. We've stood in wretched lines for hours, watching hundreds of people bypass us and be allowed in. Then, right before we were going to die of hypothermia from the skimpy clothing we wore, some promoter would walk the line, point at us, jerk his thumb, and say, "You two." It was bizarre.

As happy as I was to be getting in, I always felt a little guilty about all the people in front of us still waiting (who may or may not ever be allowed in) and the line buddies we made in our immediate vicinity. Reverberating through my head were the voices of all my elementary school teachers yelling, "Charity Gaye Finnestad! No cutting! Go to the back of the line right now!"

The German and I have concluded that the only logical explanation as to why we are always eventually allowed in when so many others are not has to be our height. It was a bit of a revelation to the both of us. The very thing that made our childhood and adolescence hell was our ticket to entry in this insider world of Hollywood. We both suffered greatly from being called the Jolly Green Giant, never getting kissed, and always towering over the boys we had crushes on. Height felt like a curse. I would have sold my soul to the devil to be five-foot-four. Now, living in Tinsel Town, we could barely believe that our curse was our salvation, but it had to be. The lines possessed far more beautiful girls than us, but none were as tall. We noticed a strange phenomenon: the tall girls all walked right in. We realized we had one of the few fashionable, unpurchaseable physical commodities of our time. For the right price, you can buy just about any physical trait: bigger breasts, straighter noses, less fat, different color eyes, different color hair. What you cannot purchase, no matter how badly you want it, is height. No doctor or guru can add three to five more inches to your legs. That had to be why we were always let in. We were in possession of something in limited supply that has high value in our modern society.

Going on that theory, the German and I wondered. If we acted confident and walked straight to the front of the line instead of waiting for hours, we might be let right in. We wondered if, by the luck of the gene pool, we might have the correct image to expect welcome and entry into the insider club. Maybe the reason we always had to stand in line forever was because we walked to the back of it and expected that we should. What if we were to pretend we were important and walk to the front expecting to be let in? Would they call us out for our arrogance, send us to the back, and never let us in again, or would they fling open the velvet rope and invite us into the inner sanctum?

It would be a risky move. It might mean pissing off the door guy and being blackballed from all the fun parties. It also might mean no more lines! It was audacious and bold. But why not be bold? Everyone else in this town was faking it. You know the expression, "fake it until you make it"? It's a required survival skill here. Illusion, and your ability to create the right illusion, will get you much further than substance. If you think about it, the entire town is built on an industry of illusion. It shows. Everything here is a dog-and-pony show, and everyone from waiters, to lawyers, to doctors, to agents, to pizza delivery guys have a bit of an actor in them. They may not be working in the movie industry, but they're touched by it and have to perform at a certain level just to survive here. This has a terrible effect on the relationships between people. You practically have to become a human lie detector to know whom to trust. Even then, you are bound to make mistakes, and when you do, the emotional costs can be devastating. This is why a lot of folks say that Hollywood is a lonely city, despite the masses of people who live here. Many of the inhabitants become so adept at playing the game and putting on the show that they forget their own humanity.

I do not believe illusion is a completely bad thing, though. Nor do I think caring about image is wrong. In fact, I think illusion can be one of the great joys of existence. It gives us an escape from the monotony of our everyday lives. It's the reason we read books and watch movies. It's what inspired all the great artists, musicians, and visionaries throughout time. Illusion is the spice in our everyday life, and image is the sugar. That's right—image sweetens the deal.

The trick is, you can't care about it more than substance, and many people in this town lose their grip on that reality. It occurs quickly, and people don't even know it has happened. They think they still have their integrity and substance, but somewhere along the way, they trade it in to look cooler. The insanity of vanity takes over, and they quit caring about all the things that mattered to them before. Looking good becomes more important than being good. This is the eternal sickness that plagues Hollywood, but it is also this mastery of illusion and image that makes it great.

The German yanks me forward.

I'm ripped out of my musings and almost off my four-inch heels. My legs quake with terror as we approach the Dragon Lady. What are we doing? She's staring at us with what can only be described as ice cold X-ray vision. I cringe. This is social suicide. She's going to hate us forever. She does the very best parties in town. We can kiss them all good-bye. Not only does she have a heart of ice, she also has the memory of an elephant. She will hold this against us for our entire existence. If we can even manage to exist here without being driven out by her Perfect Police within the month. She has them everywhere.

Oh, why didn't we just stay in our place? The line. The back of the line, in fact.

I want to cry. I knew it. Pride goeth before the fall. The oldest lesson in the book, and I had to screw it up. I steel myself for the verbal assault and public humiliation we are about to endure. I clutch the German's hand. At least I will have company in purgatory.

"What's taking so long, Dave? Open that thing and let these ladies in."

I watch in slow motion as the Dragon Lady's lips bark out the unexpected command. Her minion pulls back the velvet rope.

Holy shit! It worked! We're in! We don't have to wait in line.

The German squeezes my hand in a silent command to stay calm and strut.

It's all I can do not to burst into a Yippy Skippy, my happiness dance that resembles an Irish jig on crack. But that would never do. I may know the value of celebrating the little victories, but I also know the value of pretending you're such a cool cat that you don't give a shit. In Hollywood, everyone who makes it pretends it was an accident and that they could care less. "Luck and good fortune," they say in interviews, decrying their own talent and driving ambition. Everyone knows that open-faced ambition is considered ugly, and pride in one's work is considered bad form, so instead, a casual tone of humble worship of the god of luck marks their public persona.

Even though I'm highly emotional and exuberant by nature and would love to burst into a Yippy Skippy, sharing my joy with whomever happens to be inside the hallowed sanctuary of coolness, I've learned to act as nonchalant and blasé as the next girl when the situation calls for it. And traversing through hot-shot parties with the rich and famous definitely calls for it.

Who would have thunk it? The German and I are officially insiders. Sure, we don't deserve this, as it is based on completely superficial things, but neither do more than half of the people in here. Besides, this isn't the end for us. This is just the beginning. Someday, we really are going to do something with substance that impacts the world and makes it a better place. But until that glorious day arrives, we're going to fake it with the best of them and have a damn good time doing it!

Opting for an internal Yippy Skippy, I strut the bored Walk of Entitlement into the building and into a whole new world of wonder.

Whoo-hoo! Let's hit the dance floor!

Fake-amous Identity [fāk-ā-mes ī-**den**-tə-tē]
noun

1. An alter ego that one assumes when pretending to be someone famous.

2. A means to gain entry into clubs of the moment in LA.

Example: Her fake-amous identity as Cher's niece garnered her a goodie bag at the *People* magazine party.

THE REAL IMPOSTOR

I'm cruising along at a steady pace on the foot trail that runs along the Pacific Ocean between Santa Monica and Temescal Canyon. I'm wearing a big red hat to protect my face from the blazing sun and oversized glasses to keep out the blinding glare. My iPod's blasting Tina Turner's "Simply the Best." I smell the salt water in the air and revel in the refreshing breeze coming off the ocean.

Suddenly, out of the corner of my eye, I see a dozen Japanese tourists running toward me. Their cameras are clicking away and fanny packs are bouncing. They're yelling, wild with excitement. I turn to see which celebrity behind me is causing all the commotion. There's no one. In fact, there is nothing in the vicinity of their mad charge, except for me. Like a deer in the headlights, I freeze. Then it registers; they think I'm someone else.

Panicking, I start to run. This only incites them further. Like a bunny rabbit fleeing a pack of rabid coyotes, I tear down the ocean trail, red sunhat flapping and a stream of Japanese tourists trailing behind. Let me tell you, Red Bull doesn't give you wings—fear does. Never in all my days have I moved as fast as this. Finally, right before my lungs burst, I start to gain some distance between myself and the star-struck tourists. Thank god they aren't tall Norwegians, or I'd be in real trouble. I'm not exactly in racing condition, but thanks to those extra four inches of height, I'm gaining ground.

I get to my car and do a James Bond-style dive into the safety of the Little Pip. I turn and realize that the tourists quit chasing me at least a half a mile ago. Since then I've been running like a bat out of hell from my own shadow.

Acting as if it is perfectly normal to approach one's vehicle in such a terror-stricken fashion, I do what every embarrassed Hollywood-ite would do in such a situation—I pull out my phone and pretend I'm getting an important call. That'll shut down all the curious and amused glances being shot my way.

It doesn't take a genius to figure out that my overall look screamed celebrity to the tourists. What they don't realize is that no real-life celebrity would be wearing something as flashy as my red hat, nor would they ever be out alone in tourist hell (aka Santa Monica). Celebs camouflage themselves in everyday life. Only normal people, like me, get to have a highly individual style and not fear the attention-grabbing nature of it.

When I first moved here, I didn't understand the way it worked either. I remember approaching the German at The Lounge and telling her a guy who looked and sounded an awful lot like a Famous Actor had just tried to pick me up. She laughed and informed me it *was* the Famous Actor. Well, if it was the real Famous Actor, where was his spotlight, and why the fuck was he so incognito? Then I began to realize that all celebrities are. Only a few, like Paris and J-Lo, actually ham it up and want the attention. Most are in hiding.

This essentially means that the people dressed to kill at the clubs, bars, and restaurants are the normal people, and the scruffy-looking rats are the celebs. It's very confusing to newbies and tourists. I can't blame them. What makes it even more confusing are the Real Impostors. These should not be confused with the Look-Alikes who perform bad television dressed as Britney Spears. The Real Impostor is the Joe Blow or Jane Doe who wears Celebrity Gear at the clubs (like hats, hoodies, sunglasses, and homeless kid attire) pretending to be incognito when actually they're screaming, "I'm one of them, notice me!"

Please note, ladies and gents—one quick way of detecting a Real Impostor is by observing their location. If the beautiful-faced, street thug-attired, Ray-Ban-sporting, hoodie-covered fellow is sitting at a table, he may or may not be an actual celeb. If, however, he is lounging against the bar, he is definitely the Real Impostor. Celebs can afford a table.

Holding the phone in my trembling hand, I decide I'd better make an actual call, or I'm going to look even more ridiculous than I already do. Dialing my baby brother, Squirt, back in Oregon, I give him the rundown on what just took place. Laughing his ass off, he tries to figure out who they could have possibly thought I was. He concludes I can't be J-Lo, because my ass is too small (he does have a point). I can't be Julia Roberts, because my mouth isn't big enough (odd; he always used to call me Big Mouth). I can't be Madeleine Stowe, because I'm *way* too young (how sweet). I can't be Jennifer Love Hewitt, because I'm far too intelligent (how they were supposed to determine that at a glance is beyond me, but god bless Squirt for esteeming my intellect). Then he delivers the sucker punch I should have known was coming after all that flattery: "I got it! You're the new and improved Michael Jackson!"

Laughter blasts through the line and nearly blows out my eardrum. Pretending to be offended, as is expected of me, I laugh on the inside. There's no chance of me ever pretending to be something I'm not with my brother. He will burst my ego bubble right down to the concrete in a heartbeat if I ever become too big for my britches. Guess I'm stuck being the plain old real Charity.

But I gotta say, rumors are, "I'm *huge* in Japan!"

Top 10 Love Stories I Recommend
Borrowing from the Library of Life,
But NOT Purchasing…

"First Love"
"Second Love"
"The Bad Boy"
"The Tortured Artist"
"Small Brain, Big Cock"
"A Foreign Affair"
"The Father Figure"
"Fast and Furious"
"One Night to Remember"
"A Two-for-One Special"

LOANER LOVE

I raise my hand to knock on the door. Before I even touch it, it flings open, and there he stands in the doorway: the Big One, my lover of the last several months. And he's buck naked!

I can't help but laugh. Who answers the door buck naked? Without cracking a smile or saying a word, he slings me over his shoulder and carries me up two flights of stairs. I giggle hysterically the whole way. It feels like a cheesy scene from a dime-store romance novel. I wait for him to laugh, but he doesn't utter a sound. We get to his room. He tosses me on the bed, rips up my skirt, and drives his cock into my peach-ca. I don't feel silly anymore. This is hot! I've never felt so alive! I explode in an orgasm. He's not done. He rolls me over and continues. My fingers grasp the bedspread, holding on for the ride. The only thing in the whole world that exists is his perfect cock. I explode again. He explodes. We tumble together to the floor in a pile of sated bliss. Wrapping his arms around me and cradling me on his chest, he tenderly kisses my forehead and says the most dreaded words in the whole English language.

"I love you."

Oh shit! I freeze. Now what? Clearly the German was wrong with her, "Stop worrying. Men in this town don't fall in love" speech. Next he'll want a white picket fence and me wearing a cupcake dress while uttering ball-and-chain-until-eternity vows. How did this happen?

Three months ago, when I decided I was ready to take the plunge into the Wild West world of dating in Tinsel Town, I made a decision. I was ready for romance and passion—in fact, I was desperately in need of both—but I was not even close to ready for commitment and love. This little birdie had just flown the cage a short time ago. I needed some time to test my wings before I met a fellow flier, let alone signed a lease on a tree branch and built a nest with one.

I did, however, crave connection. I needed to be touched. It had been so long since I'd been with a man that I was afraid my equipment might not work anymore. I wondered if it was still under lease and could be returned for new parts if that was the case.

The truth was, I hadn't been with anyone since my ex-husband, and during the last two years I was with him, he made love to me a total of two times a year. Yes, I really did say four times in two years.

I wanted sex. Correction: I needed sex. I was pretty sure I was missing out on one of the huge joys of being human. My Christian upbringing had pounded the belief into my head that sex outside of marriage was bad. That ridiculous philosophy had trapped me into two unhealthy marriages because I had a little thing called a healthy sex drive. If I hadn't had that belief, I would have just slept with them and moved on when the relationships died of natural causes, like normal people do. No. Instead I suffered for years and years trying to keep a dead thing alive because I'd worn a white dress in front of hundreds of people and made promises driven by hormones.

It was time to shed my antiquated beliefs about sex (along with all the other pre-packaged beliefs that come with organized religion) so that I could find out what really worked for me, and not what worked for some writers communicating with primitive tribes in the desert thousands of years ago.

When I shared my thoughts with the German, she was shocked. "You've slept with how many men?"

"I told you, three."

"Really? Ever?"

I nodded.

"Does that count 'Clinton' style?"

I nodded again.

"And you were married to two of them?" she shrieked.

"Yes."

"My god. You need to get laid!"

"Exactly."

I was pretty sure I needed a good dose of mind-boggling, rocket-riding sex. I'd never had it before, but the evidence out there suggested it existed and could be discovered if one was willing to experiment. I certainly was. It was time to learn about myself and the world through passionate moments. I wanted to taste, try, and touch my way into being a fully evolved human being.

"There's only one problem," I informed the German. "I want sex and romance without love and commitment." At that point she almost fell off her chair laughing.

"You're really too much, Charity. Where did you come from?"

Okay, let's be honest. I knew there would be a little love. I could never be with someone I didn't love a little, but what I didn't want was to let passion trap me in a relationship before I'd fully worked out my relationship with myself. I would secretly love them, but not ask for their love in return.

"Seriously, I've been thinking about it, and I believe the only possible approach to prevent it from getting messy is absolute honesty right from the get-go."

By this point the German was convulsed with laughter. "Dare I ask? What *exactly* do you plan to say?"

Getting a little miffed that she was not taking me seriously, I informed her, "I was thinking something like, 'I'm looking for a lover, but please don't fall in love with me.'"

Diet Coke sprayed out of the German's nose, and she actually fell off her chair. Gasping for air, she declared, "Oh my god, I love you!"

When she finished her epileptic-like seizure on the floor, the German reassured me it wasn't going to be hard to convince a guy to buy into unlimited sex with no strings attached. "Men in LA do not fall in love," she declared. Indeed, she felt my whole approach was over-thought and unnecessary. She highly recommended forgoing any type of relationship and just hooking up with sexy strangers for nights of unbridled passion. I informed her that wouldn't work. I needed familiar and safe, just not permanent. I was on a mission to find the guy who could give me both, and earth-shattering orgasms on top of it.

"Well if that's what you want, that's what we'll get you." The German insisted it wouldn't be difficult, and once again reassured me, "You don't have anything to worry about. Men in LA don't—"

"Fall in love. I know, I know," I retorted. "I heard you the first time, but I'm not convinced. They can't be that different from men in Oregon, and they fell in love with me on a regular basis." This sent the German into another gale of laughter. When she could breathe again, she raised her Diet Coke and toasted, "Here's to getting you properly fucked as quickly as possible—you clearly need it!"

We were three weeks into my newly formed quest for a casual lover when I met the Big One. The backdrop was the Parking Violations Bureau on Pico Boulevard. I know. Not exactly a romantic setting for the beginning of an affair. Jayne Ann Krentz would be mortified. But beggars can't be choosers, and I was definitely in the beggar category. Meeting an affair-worthy fellow in Tinsel Town was proving harder than the German and I'd originally estimated. It wasn't that there weren't plenty of men interested in monkey business—it was just that their approach to romance seemed decidedly twisted.

It had become an ongoing joke among the German and I that there was no such thing as free sex in LA. Everything had a price. If the sexual climate of the Big Apple could be compared to a high school dance where passions were ignited and then acted on, Tinsel Town could be compared to a strip club where the goodies were presented in a tempting display and then pulled away until you paid the right price to touch. No joke. Sex was commonly used as a commodity in Hollywood; it was not a natural explosion of passion, lust, or love. New York had the Stock Exchange, and LA had the Pussy Exchange.

The entire entertainment industry was built from the ground up on the "sex sells" philosophy. It infiltrated everything. It was not just limited to business. People lived and breathed their work. It didn't stop when they went out and played. In fact, mixing business and social climbing was an absolute must. They'd barter what they could offer you (or pretend to offer you) against what they could get from you. As a result, you couldn't socialize and party in this town for long without learning the nature of human interaction and your personal market value.

It was a fascinating phenomenon. Girls ended up having no choice but to take one of two roads to their sexuality being treated as a commodity. They either went by the "what is rare has more value" philosophy, or played very hard to get so they wouldn't be thought of as cheap. (Which in some cases forced them to say no and repress their natural instincts, even when they would like to say yes, because they couldn't afford an easy girl reputation.) Or, they tried to prove their nymph-dom by showing off their sexuality and putting out for everyone who offered them something (connections, prestige, presents, film parts, etc.), thinking that their obvious sexuality would increase their value. (Men really dug manipulating that group. It was so much fun to use a girl's insecurity against her.) Sadly, both ways of operating were unnatural and decidedly unfulfilling when it came to sex and relationships. Both operated against natural inclinations.

There I was, finally ready for the first time in my life to try out a casual affair, and confronting a sexual commodities market. I detested the thought of engaging in commerce in bed. I was all for unlicensed hanky-panky—I just wasn't up for using anyone or being used. I needed a nice, normal guy who wasn't heavily involved in this ridiculous world. But where was I going to find one of those? Certainly not at the sexy clubs and parties the German and I had been attending.

Nope. It would be there, at the Parking Violations Bureau on Pico Boulevard, where the German and I were waiting in a ridiculously long line to give our hard-earned money away to the city of LA for undeserved parking tickets—the bane of my existence. Who would have guessed those stupid parking tickets would turn out to be my sexual salvation?

As the German and I impatiently waited for our number to be called, a beautiful specimen of rugged, Dutch-Zimbabwean manhood strolled into the utilitarian government office. The temperature in the room jumped a good ten degrees, and both the German and I lost our ability to blink. Even the eighty-year-old granny next to us couldn't take her eyes off him. He had the whole package: curly blonde hair, a mischievous little boy smile, and the naughtiest golden tiger eyes I'd ever seen. Unabashedly, he brandished all of his male energy at the German and me, not even trying to downplay perusing us up and down. He was a man who was hot and knew it.

Then he made his move. My heart pounded as the Big One approached us. I could feel beads of sweat forming on my palms with each step he took in our direction.

"Number seventy-six. Number seventy-six," blasted over the intercom.

I looked down. Wouldn't you know it; that was my number. Just my luck!

On lead feet, I made my way to the cashier window, dejected. I glanced back and saw the Big One engaged in an animated conversation with the German. No doubt he would fall madly in love with her while I forked over my hard-earned cash. Was the whole bloody world conspiring to keep me from getting laid?

After the clerk handed me my receipt, I headed back to the two most beautiful people in the room. When I reached them, the Big One informed me that he had consulted with the German and would be taking the two of us to lunch after he paid his tickets. When his number was called, the German gave me the scoop.

Apparently he had walked up and said, "Your friend's hot. What do you think my chances are?" She'd told him, 100 percent. After slugging her for throwing me under the bus, I squeezed her hand with happiness. Oh my god, it was really going to happen.

As promised, the curly blonde god took us to the Apple Pan, where we had a casual laugh-a-minute lunch. By the end, he had made a date with me for a hike that Saturday. I love hiking, and I loved hiking with him even more. On Sunday, the Big One was even kind enough to help me move into the new little cottage I'd signed a lease on the week before. What a great week. The German got her bed back to herself, and I found a chivalrous man. Clearly this was exactly the right guy to try casual romance with. I just didn't know how to break the rules of the game to him.

I agonized about the conversation. I practiced over and over how I would say it: "I want your body, your friendship, and your affection, but not your heart? Please, whatever you do, don't fall in love with me, because this is temporary." I thought he would be appalled. What kind of person goes into a relationship telling that much of the truth? You were supposed to dance, deceive, and shock them when you left. The German said that was what men did, but I couldn't do it. Breaking my own heart would be one thing; breaking someone else's would be another thing altogether. I didn't do well with guilt. He would have to be told.

That Tuesday, I sat across the table from him at Johnny Rockets on Melrose and gave him the unvarnished version of how things would go down between us if we slept together. Imagine my surprise when he nearly jumped out of his seat with excitement.

"You mean I get to screw one of the hottest girls I've ever met, whenever I want, and I don't have to woo her and pretend to be in love with her to accomplish it?"

"Well yes, I guess you could put it like that. The main thing is, I don't want you to fall in love with me."

"Are you serious? I've hit the fucking jackpot! This is the arrangement every guy dreams of. No commitment, seriously? Is this some kind of trick?"

"Well, geez, I didn't expect you to be quite so enthusiastic about not falling in love with me. I am pretty lovable. But yes, that is the deal. No commitment. No trick."

"I'm in!"

And boy, oh boy, was he! That man was inside my body faster than I could say, "Check."

The German was right. My requirements weren't a problem. By Friday, we had fucked, laughed, screwed, hiked, sucked, and danced our way through every major landmark in LA. The man was an animal. I'd never been with anyone who had such an insatiable need for sex. It was possible that he even thought about sex more than I did, and I thought about it all the time. That's what happened when you'd faced years of deprivation. And he didn't just think about it, he acted. He took me on the bench on top of Runyan Canyon. He bent me over and took me on the Will Rogers trail in Malibu. He took me on the wet sand of El Matador Beach. In the elevator of the Standard Hotel. In the bathroom of Saddle Ranch. The back of my car. The front of my car. The hood of my car. With one leg under my car.

By the end of three months, we had sexually christened all of greater LA. There was nowhere I could go without a memory of an orgasm. My eternal drought had ended. I was a goddess. A nymph. A slut. A wild woman. Quite simply, I was happy.

What I was not, though, was in love.

Sure, he flipped all of my sexual switches, but I was a lot more complex than that. I had mental, emotional, and spiritual switches that would have to be flipped to "all stations go" before I would even think about falling in love.

I thought of him as a library book. He wasn't the kind of book I had to buy the minute I cracked him open to make a part of my home library, but he was a darn fine read for a loaner. I would always remember the story with him, but I didn't need to read it again or keep it. When we were finished, I would return him to the library of life and check out another.

"Are you going to say anything?"

I'm jerked back into the present. Looking into the exotic tiger eyes of the man who has given me the best sex of my life, I'm totally frustrated. I feel like screaming, "Why did you have to say that and ruin everything?" I sadly realize the story has to end. I can't be responsible for leading him on past this point.

I suppose it was inevitable. Here is a man who is charm embodied. Women adore him. Women pursue him. Women literally throw themselves at him. When we are out to dinner, women approach him when I'm in the bathroom to try and pick him up. I've never seen a playboy with such honey-to-the-bees energy in my life. He's gotten used to running from, instead of chasing, women. He feels like every girl wanted to trap and tie him down. He isn't sure he's tasted everything out there and wants to keep his options open.

Then I come along. For the first time in his life, here's a girl saying, "I don't want anything from you but sex and friendship. Please don't fall in love with me."

It's like waving a red flag to a bull. His natural hunting instincts kick in, and he has the novel experience of being the hunter, not the hunted, which confuses him into thinking he loves me. If he really thinks about it, he'll know I'm not right for him. We are as different as night and day, and our values are, too. I would make his life a living hell if I was actually trying to build a future with him. He's too used to low-maintenance girls who live to serve him. That sure as hell isn't me. I expect a partnership. If I said yes, he'd be getting a lot more than he bargained for. He'd be unhappy, and he'd make me unhappy in no time flat. Our story works because of the way it is written. It wouldn't work another way.

Lying here, listening to him declare his love for me and the implicated desire to build a future, I know all this—and if he's really honest with himself, I suspect he does, too. I don't think he'll be that honest, though. I think the fine story is more magical for him if he adds me to his personal legend as the one that got away. In his mind, I'll be the only shot he had at happiness in a relationship. The thing is, it's a fantasy relationship. Not a real one.

Pulling down my skirt and kissing his forehead, I climb out of the tangle of limbs we are on his bedroom floor. "I love you, too, but we aren't right for each other."

"I disagree," he says.

"Please don't make this harder than it is. You knew the rules. I'm not ready for love, but I promise I'll never forget you."

I won't ruin his story by dousing it in truth. He has loaned me an amazing adventure, and I'll let him keep his tragic romance if that's what he wishes.

Picking up my panties, I wait to hear if he has anything else he needs to say. He just stares at me in silence. I feel so bad I want to cry. I guess casual affairs aren't for me after all. Men in LA do fall in love.

"I'm so sorry. I tried to prevent this from happening," I whisper. "Please don't hate me forever."

Turning, I slowly walk down the two flights of stairs I was carried up moments earlier. At the bottom, I find the heels that fell off when he picked me up.

As I walk out the door, my heart is heavy and my spirit is sad, but I must admit—my body has never felt better.

Mental Mudslide [**men**-tl **məd**-slīd]
noun
1. A psychological condition resembling the houses that slide off the hills in LA whenever there is a deluge. It's generally believed to be caused by the failure to obtain a desired goal. Symptoms include, but are not limited to tears, an uncontrollable desire to sleep, and an overall apathy about life.

Example: "Within hours of feeling at the top of her game, a mental mudslide hit her, and now she's sobbing into her vino."

KEEP SHAKING THAT ASS

It's the end of another day. I slip out of my favorite red heels, stretch my cramped, aching toes, and fling my utterly exhausted, slightly intoxicated, five-foot-ten-inch frame onto my much-loved bed. I have to admit, warts and all, I'm hopelessly in love with Hollywood. Like the Wild West in the days of old, it is a place where anything can happen. Today was a perfect example.

This afternoon, I had a callback for a high-paying commercial that could have really saved me from my current financial predicament—which is just a fancy way of saying my broke-ass state. For those of you who aren't familiar with Hollywood lingo, a callback means that I already went to the audition, and they really liked me. Now they're trying to narrow it down to their absolute favorite. The star of this particular commercial promises to be rather unusual: a pair of legs strutting around in heels.

With my head in the clouds, I foolishly decided to take the 405 freeway to my callback, which today of all days resembled a parking lot. No matter. I was so confident about booking the job that I wasn't even worried about being late. I don't normally count on a job before it's mine, but this one was different. Not to brag, but I have a great set of legs—and besides, I already took a look at the other girls at the first audition, and there was no competition. Staying in first gear for ten grueling miles, I counted the palm trees marching by and tried not to crash into the brake-happy driver in front of me, all the while belting out Janis Joplin tunes at the top of my lungs.

After an hour of moving slower than molasses, I finally reached the casting studio. I rushed in past dozens of nervous actors, all preparing for auditions. I found my sign-in location. Much to my dismay, my tardiness meant the other girls had taken all the shoes in my size, and I would be forced to wear four-inch heels that would fit Shaquille O'Neal. Wobbling into the casting room, I was faced with a sizable crowd. There was the casting director, the client, six competing girls, three unidentified stooges, and Julio, a flaming gay Latino who introduced himself as the choreographer.

Choreographer? My stomach dropped. No one mentioned anything about choreography. As I watched Julio orchestrate dance moves I could never hope to remember, my dreams of booking this spot and securing next month's rent started to crumble around me. I flashed back to when I was twelve years old and had my first growth spurt, only to discover a pair of arms and legs that were too long for me and completely out of my control. Yes, my nickname was chopsticks, and no, I didn't like it!

Trying to get a grip on my growing insecurity, I teetered through the steps in my monster shoes. After two run-throughs, Julio decided we were ready and told one of the stooges to hit the music. We began the salsa with sixteen sets of eyes on us. Right, right, left, left, twist, dip, kick. Just as we were nearing the finale and relief was setting in, it happened. My two-sizes-too-big heel slipped right out from under me. The only thing falling faster than my ass to the stage was my pride, and any last chance of booking the job. As I walked out of the casting studio, my bum bruised, my dignity in shreds, and my mind now worried about how I would pay the rent, my phone chirped.

It was an invitation from my buddy, Double O Seven, to a party at his best friend No Boundaries's house. Double O Seven, a man known and loved by more women than any man I've ever met, has a gift: introduce him to a beautiful woman, and five minutes later, he has a fan. I should know; I'm the head of his fan club. Thinking that maybe a party was just what I needed, I accepted.

When I got home from my devastating audition, I did what every hardworking writer/model does to cope with such setbacks. I took a nap. That's right. I thumbed my nose at the brilliant sunshine and life happening all around Hollywood and crawled into bed to lick my wounds. The bum-bruising fall had taken its toll on my spirit as well as my ass. Modeling may only be a means to pay the bills until I achieve my real goal of being a published writer, but if I don't book jobs, I don't eat. Feeling antisocial and blue after waking up from my nap, I sent Double O Seven a text. *What happens if I bail tonight?*

His response: *Get your cute little ass up here!*

Not wanting to be a flake, I decided I better go. Outfitting myself in battle gear—lipstick, heels, and the tiniest miniskirt ever invented (an absolute psychological necessity after my humiliating fall)—I prepared to enter the fray. Making my way up the windy road to No Boundaries's pad, I attempted to find my inner party girl, but to no avail. I simply couldn't get over the feeling of anxiety. How was I going to make it until my writing took off? Am I crazy for even trying for something so hard to obtain? Everyone is constantly telling me I'm a dreamer. And they're right. I am. But don't you have to be to accomplish something great? Or am I just wasting my time dreaming my life away? It's so hard to know sometimes.

No Boundaries's pad was the home of a true connoisseur. A combination of European design meets cutting-edge technology, his place was absolutely stunning. To my rent-worried mind, it was another planet. When I walked in, No Boundaries was screening breathtaking underwater footage of his most recent trip on his super-size yacht for a half a dozen friends. We saw him scuba diving with eels, sharks, and other exotic wild sea creatures. The Greek Heir arrived and gave No Boundaries a huge hug and a happy birthday wish. It was at that moment I realized that this was not just another No Boundaries after-party. It was, in fact, his birthday.

Soon other guests began pouring in. We all hopped into a cable-car elevator that reminded me of the one at the *Sacré-Coeur* in Paris and descended to the music studio below the main house. Composed entirely of glass and steel, the LA skyline sparkled below like an ocean of lights. There was even a fully equipped stage at the far end of the room. Grabbing a vodka tonic from the passing waiter, I watched as No Boundaries, with a few friends in tow, casually climbed onto the stage and grabbed a guitar. Thus the night officially began.

Clearly this computer wizard who built a technological empire has always secretly dreamt of being a rock star. Tonight, he was a rock-and-roll god. The performance was nothing short of brilliant. Kicking into the next song, he really let loose. Dancing around the stage, grinning like a schoolboy and ripping away at his instrument, this mild-mannered computer genius was transformed.

As he shook it up, I shaped up. Surrendering to the moment, I let the music and the energy of the night carry me away. In no time flat, my face hurt from smiling, my booty hurt from shaking, and my lungs hurt from screaming. The joy of life coming off No Boundaries was palpable and completely contagious. I was getting the contact high of my life, with no drugs involved.

In true Hollywood style, a realization came to me: I might have fallen on my ass that morning, but tonight I was shaking that very same ass to the music of somebody living out his dreams. Before me on the stage was a man who had started with nothing, but with hard work and determination, he had changed life on the planet for all of us. Here he was now, living out his teenage fantasy with me and twenty-four other friends. If that isn't what it's all about in this Wild West town, I don't know what is. Sure, we have more than our fair share of shysters, illusionists, and dreamers who will never accomplish their goals, but we also have a few brilliant visionaries with the brains, guts, and determination to realize their ambitions.

Back home in the fairy cottage, as I kick off my red heels and drift off to sleep, I can't help thinking about my own life. Maybe, just maybe, if I keep dreaming, keep getting up after I fall, keep laughing at myself, keep shaking my ass, and keep trying, someday I, too, will see my writing ambitions fulfilled and will be belting out Janis Joplin songs at my fifty-third birthday for a circle of my closest friends. Although that day is a long way off, one can't help but think that if it's going to happen anywhere, it is going to be here in the Land of Dreams.

Von Trapp-alike [von-**trap**-ə-līk]
adjective

1. Having a similar quality of character to Captain von Trapp from *The Sound of Music*. In other words: tall, dark, slightly overbearing, confident, expects people to jump when he whistles, wears power like a second skin, stands up for his ideals, has a secret soft side and big heart.
2. The type of man Charity Gaye Finnestad is madly attracted to.

Example: "He was such a Von Trapp-alike that her heart melted."

JUST SHOW, NEVER TELL

"Did you hear that O.J. Simpson has a team of investigators working to assemble the exact same jury he had for his first trial?"

The table burst into laughter. I can't believe it. He reads Andy Borowitz (borowitzreport.com), my favorite political satirist. Turning to Mr. Well-Read, a smart and funny businessman who is seated next to me at the dinner party, I applaud him on his taste in bloggers. We proceed to engage in an entertaining conversation, and I realize that I have just found a new friend in Tinsel Town. I don't feel any sexual chemistry with him, but I definitely like the way his brain works. Wait a minute; he would be perfect for my friend, Stunt Girl. I'll have to make sure they meet.

The dinner party comes to an end and he offers to walk me to my car. When we get to the car, I tell him what a pleasure it was to meet him, and that we should hang soon. I'm very clear with my physical distance and casual way of speaking that I mean as friends, not romantically. Before I can climb into the Little Pip and leave, the poor fellow suffers a complete brain meltdown and breaks the cardinal rule between men and women.

Opening his mouth and inserting his size-seven shoe (okay, I'm just guessing with the size thing, but he does only come up to my waist), he informs me that he really likes me and wants to be friends, but he feels I should know a little something-something first. Apparently, he is an amazing lover and he knows how to do this one little trick that makes every woman scream. He finds me attractive, so he's willing to demonstrate it for me if I've never experienced it. Just in case I'm not sold on the idea, he explains it in graphic detail. I stand there, my skin crawling with embarrassment and discomfort. I mentally cross him off the candidate list for Stunt Girl. I want to yell, "Don't you know, Romeo? Never, ever, ever, ever, for any reason, or at any time, ever, brag about your sexual prowess to a woman! Especially not as a last-ditch effort to get a girl who is clearly not attracted to you into bed!"

It seems that a lot of men do not know this unwritten rule, so I'm writing it down. I don't care what you can do, even if you are Don Juan himself. Even if you have made women faint, scream, or cry like babies. Even if you have converted a hundred lesbians into cock-loving whores. Even if there are women with posters of your tongue hanging above their beds. Even if you have had to make molds of your cock for desperate fans who cannot bear to touch anyone else's since they have had yours. In other words, even if you are god's gift to the finer sex, you never tell a woman how great you are in bed; under no circumstances, at no time, with no exceptions. Do you hear me?

I'm not kidding here, guys. I know you think I'm exaggerating, but trust me, I'm not! Every single time a guy boasts about his hanky-panky skills, he is actually advertising his total ineptitude. I know men are competitive and have an overwhelming desire to brag about anything they think they've done well. I also realize that we live in an advertisement-based culture. Combine these two things and I understand why you might get the misguided impression that publicly posting your game stats is a good idea—but I can assure you, it is not!

Every girl knows that attraction, sex, and coming are a case-by-case thing. We know that all of us are radically different, and that what gets one off will not work for the next. We know, because we talk. You would be shocked at the graphic honesty of our conversations. There is not a magic button, boys. It's different for every girl. Sure, being on top and a little finger move worked for Suzie Q, but I can promise you it won't work for Mary Jane. She hates the finger trick, prefers you on top, and comes when you pull her hair. Get my drift?

Meanwhile, any fellow who brags about his sexual prowess with women as a collective is clearly making a ton of false assumptions. He is totally insensitive to the individuality of the female orgasm. He has no clue with his preconceived ideas of how to connect with you and discover your button. Also, he is so attached to his own perception of himself as a stud that he probably has no idea that the women with him just faked it to get him to stop.

It draws to mind a dinner party I was at a year ago where a Peacock announced to the table at large that every woman he ever slept with had no less than three orgasms, every time. If that wasn't enough, he also claimed that he never had a "lovemaking session" (his words, not mine) that lasted less than an hour. As he uttered the statement, a mental picture popped into my head: him on top of a chick pumping, her looking at the clock over his shoulder and thinking, "Christ, I already faked three and it's been an hour, will this never end?"

It was just too much. I burst into laughter and nearly choked on my drink.

Now as I look at Mr. Well-Read, this self-proclaimed Lothario standing in front of me, I think someone really needs to tell these poor souls to close their traps. It isn't show-and-tell, boys. You just show; you never tell. If the window to show is not opening for you, then trust me, laying out a laundry list of your qualifications for the job is not going to do the trick either. It just makes you look like a desperate schmuck. Better to keep your mouth shut and walk away with the secret knowledge that you would have been the best lover she ever had (which clearly makes it her loss if it's true) than to make yourself look like an ignorant fool. Trust me, the really good lovers know this. They never tell anyone.

It just oozes out of their being, and they intuitively know how to show you with their actions. So come on, boys, leave us wondering. Or if you see the opportunity, show us, but please, no more ad campaigns.

FYI... for those of you who are utterly compelled to orate on your sexual techniques, there is one time a man can tell a woman (that he has not previously fucked) what he is going to do to her: when you are lying in bed with her, with the very real possibility of taking her. Then, by all means, go for it. Here's your chance to get all your bragging out. Give her a verbal blow-by-blow of the exquisite torture you will enact upon her lovely body. She'll be even hotter than she already was. Just be sure it's not a resume of what you have done to other women, or you can say good-bye to a happy ending. Remember, it's you and her, not you and your history as god's gift to womankind.

Names I've been called (in chronological order):

Pumpkin	*I enjoyed a butterball physique until the age of two.*
Gumby	*So sue me, I'm double-jointed.*
Toothpick	*Toothpicks have feelings too!*
Bookworm	*Okay, you got me there.*
Nerd	*Better that than being a bully like you.*
Geek	*What is the difference between that and nerd anyway?*
Chopsticks	*Would you like it if I called you an object you resemble?*
Poor	*I'm rich in the things that count: love, family, friends.*
Chastity	*Stop that! I said, "My name is CHARITY."*
Beaver Teeth	*Don't be cruel because I can saw wood with my front teeth.*
Brace Face	*Better than beaver teeth any day. Thanks, Mom and Dad.*
Scrawny	*Tell me something I don't know.*
Weirdo	*Normal is overrated.*
Smart	*Maybe, but being disciplined is why I got As.*
Anorexic	*I do not starve myself or throw up! I love food.*
Prude	*Seriously, because I won't sleep with you?*
Cute	*I think I'm in love.*
Slut	*Short skirts do not mean I sleep around.*
Beautiful	*My heart just smiled.*
Elegant	*Wow! Just like Audrey Hepburn? I've arrived.*

UGLY CHARITY

I hit "call" and listen to my voicemail. It's my commercial agent telling me to check my email—I have an audition today. Cool, I could use another shot at work. Sitting down at my computer, I click on the notice. I love these email audition alerts from casting companies. They give you the time, place, contact info, and a description of the character type they're looking for. In the old days (just a year ago), your agent had to try and translate a full description of what the client wanted, and you had to sit with a pen in hand scribbling as fast as you could. It sure simplifies things to get the actual description from the horse's mouth.

I glance at the screen and notice the audition time. Shit, I'm going to have to hurry—this is in an hour, and it's on the other side of town. I scroll down. Sounds fun; it's for a Sarah Silverman promo on *Comedy Central*. I will be playing a blind woman. Then I read the description of the talent they're looking for *…benign, off-kilter, and off-center talent. Certainly not mainstream and most def not attractive.* Shocked, I blink and look again. I must have misread that. Sure enough, there are the unfriendly words flashing in neon color, *…MOST DEF NOT ATTRACTIVE*. In fact, it specifically says that twice in the casting notice.

Sucking in air, I try to calm down. It can't be true? It must be a mistake. Can it possibly be? Does my agent really think I'm ugly? Picking up my phone, I speed-dial her.

"Um, I don't mean to be a pain in the ass, but are you sure I should go out for this? Did you read the description of the person they're looking for?"

My agent insists that I shouldn't take that last line so literally. It is a comedy, and she is convinced that I have comedic talent. Then in a misguided attempt to reassure me, she says, "They picked your headshot, sweetie."

Oh geez! It is worse than I thought. Not only does my agent think I'm ugly, but so do the people at The Casting Agency. What is the world coming to?

I've changed my mind. I think this email casting notice is a bad idea. In fact, I think we should abolish it altogether. Give me back the good old days when your agent candy-coated the description for you. This kind of blatant, brutal honesty is cruel and unusual punishment. What do they say when they're looking for a larger actress?

"We want an attractive fatty, def not healthy, a real Big Bertha, but make sure she has a cute face…"

I shudder to think of the psychological damage that would do, but hey, at least she knows she's still cute!

Setting down my phone, I make a decision. If I'm going to be a fugly blind woman, then I'm going to be the fugliest blind woman ever. I don't believe in doing anything halfway. Anything worth doing is worth doing well. Tearing off my normal Charity attire—pink high heels and a tiny white sundress—I begin rummaging through my closet looking for "def not attractive," blind woman attire. Finding the ugliest outfit I own (a bright green tee-shirt from an ex-boyfriend and highwater, high-waisted pants), I put it on. Then I slip on a pair of red-and-white-striped flats and part my hair down the middle. I glance in the mirror. I look like Steve Urkel meets Kris Kringle on crack. I'm ready.

America Ferrera, move over. Here comes Ugly Charity.

Bait Date [bāt dāt]

noun

1. A female who accompanies a male (usually a friend) on a date for the sole purpose of validating his date-ability to other females they may encounter throughout the course of the date.
2. An act of advertisement that endorses a man's worth.
3. The human equivalent of a juicy earthworm to a fish.

Example: "His bait date was so hot that the other girls at the concert couldn't help but wonder if he was rich, well hung, or both."

ANGEL IN BLACK

The waiter approaches and sets down what appears to be gold-plated seafood. I blink and look again. It is! The lights sparkling off of the eighteen carat-coated, aptly named Hundred Dollar Roll nearly blind me. There's more bling on the tuna than on all of the ladies at the table combined, and that's saying something, since there are eight of us and we're all dressed to kill. I look at the Man in Black and thank him once again for inviting me and the girls to join him at Koi. A true gentleman, he replies, "My pleasure."

Looking around the table at my animated friends as they pick up their pieces of the gold, I feel the stress begin to melt out of my body. Today was rough. I may live in the City of Angels, but some days it feels like I'm a permanent resident of hell.

I woke up this morning in the middle of a nightmare about fighting. A hangover, no doubt, from last night's dinner party where a judgmental, boorish, know-it-all man endeavored to give me indigestion the entire meal. When I reluctantly climbed out of bed and attempted to shake off my bad dream mojo, I realized that it was the end of May and June's rent was due in two days. Which meant that my malnourished bank account was about to get even hungrier. This was hard to imagine, since it has been sustaining on a diet that would make an anorexic look like a gluttonous pig. With that happy thought to sip my morning tea to, I felt the fire start to burn even hotter under my already well-done ass.

How was it possible that I worked twelve-hour days, never slowing down unless my body staged a protest of sickness, and I still didn't have a penny to my name? Oh yeah, that's right. I picked the artist path.

At times, it feels so bold and glorious to be blazing my own trail, creating my own destiny, writing my little heart out in Hollywood. Other times, I just feel like a complete fool for not going into law, finance, medicine—anything with a guaranteed paycheck and prestige.

Burdened by the weight of the entire world, I went into the bathroom to brush my teeth and discovered, much to my horror, that uninvited zits had decided to throw a party on my face. Geez, now I was not only broke; I was deformed, too.

Deciding it was time to get serious about making my large-scale mosaics—another risky venture that may or may not produce cashola—I headed outside to haul a seventy-pound piece of concrete up two flights of stairs. After I sat the back-breaking base on the deck where the masterpiece would be created, I began the messy process of mixing thin-set, an extra sticky version of concrete, to adhere the tiles. Unfortunately, my mind was on my bankbook, not my thin-set. Big mistake. I made the thin-set way too runny. That was just the beginning. Everything went downhill from there. In no time flat, I'd smashed my thumb with the hammer, broken the tile I was cutting in the wrong place, and totally lost my marbles.

I plopped down next to the ruined piece and started sobbing. It was the biggest pity party I'd thrown in a long time. Complete with anxiety, self-doubt, and a whole batch of "I suck."

Then I remembered, much to my horror, that tonight I'd planned another girl's night. Which meant, even though I wanted to keep the pity party going all night, I was going to have to take a two-hour vacation and pretend to be happy while entertaining the posse. I dreaded the very thought of it.

Pulling myself together enough to realize I needed to take a hike or I was never going to be able to drag myself through tonight's performance, I put on my tennis shoes. As I trudged up the hill, totally despondent, the miracle text came from the Man in Black.

Dinner at Koi?

Can't, have seven friends coming over for girl's night.

Bring them along.

So here I sit, in the dimly lit back room of Koi, feeling my spirits lift and realizing that not all angels have halos, white gowns, and wings. Sometimes you are touched by an Angel in Black. It's not that my situation is any different or that any solutions have been found, it's just that so much of life is attitude. Mine sucked today. My Angel just provided me with a much-needed readjustment. Let's face it—on a global scale, my life is pretty fabulous, stress, zits, and all. I may not have any gold in my bank account, but I'm about to have some in my belly. If that's not funny, I don't know what is.

Scooping up my piece of the gold, I lean across the table and pucker up. Clearly it's time I exchange my pity-party favors for a gratitude fest and give that Angel of mine a big fat kiss on the cheek.

INSTRUCTIONS FOR MOUNTING A BUTTERFLY:

1. Before starting, make sure the creature is completely dead. Butterflies with even a twinge of life left in them cannot be mounted.

2. After you are certain it is dead, douse the poor thing in gin or vodka to ensure the flexibility of the wings. You don't want to break off a piece of your trophy before you can even display it.

3. Next, pull the wings into the wide-open position and use an appropriately-sized board to hold them in place. Keep that beautiful object squished under the board until its wings are frozen in that position.

4. Finally stick a long, stiff object through the center of the body, pinning it to the board forever.

5. Once the butterfly is firmly in the position you desire, cover it in glass so no one else can touch it.

6. Hang and enjoy.

CAPTURED, SPREAD, AND PINNED

I look at my phone. Grrr, still no bars. Being out of contact capacity drives me bonkers. Especially when I'm waiting for a call from a man I dig, as I am right now. What I want to know is how we can figure out how to get to the moon, but we still haven't created the technology to guarantee cell phone reception in the hills of LA (Beverly, Hollywood, or Malibu). There is something wrong with this picture. Who bloody cares if we can leave footprints on the lunar landscape? What we really need is reliable communication here on terra firma.

I'm at No Boundaries's amazing pad, enjoying a lovely barbecue with a handful of friends, including the Italian Puppy, Double O Seven, and the German. Ladies and gentlemen, I'm dismayed to inform you that we, the common man of the world, aren't the only ones walking around looking for that phone sweet spot that is always out of reach. The Big Boys are fumbling around with their iPhones aloft as well. Oh, how the mighty suffer. Here I was thinking that when I finally achieved literary greatness and wealth, the nuisances of the common population would disappear. Does this mean I will still have to deal with that damn computer-generated voice when I call the phone company? The horror and suffering; an ideal fantasy world crumbling around me. Oh wait, there's a bar! Yippy Skippy!

Freezing in place without breathing for fear of breaking the connection, I wait to see if any messages come through. Sure enough, my phone lights up with several missed calls and messages: a call from my room-mate and two calls and a text message from my new crush, Too Good to Be True. Delighted, I dial him. No answer. Leaving him a voicemail, I decide maybe I better listen to my messages and see what he said. Dial. The first one is from my roommate.

"Hey Charity, that guy you like left a message that he is trying to get a hold of you, and he sounded kind of angry."

What the fuck? *Beep.* Message number two.

"Hey, I've tried your house twice, sent you two text messages, and left a voicemail on your cell. What's going on?"

My heart drops and my stomach turns. This is not normal behavior. If I'd ignored a call from him days earlier, I would possibly understand this hostile-sounding voice, but all of these calls and messages came within the last two hours. Why on earth had he gotten that worked up that fast? That's just weird. Setting down my offensive phone, a visual of how my entire relationship would play out with this fellow pops into my head.

A big white butterfly net scoops me out of the sky as I go to land on a flower and breathe in its beauty. I'm thrown into a jar and the lid is screwed on tight, with no air holes allowing me to breathe. I'm carried around by grubby fingers and displayed to all the boys in the neighbor-hood as the prize catch. Then when I die of suffocation, I'm taken out, my wings are spread apart, and my body is pinned to a trophy board where I will be held on permanent display. Isn't that how all boys like to mount their captured butterflies?

Youser! Looks like Too Good to Be True was indeed too good to be true. What a colossal disappointment. I've encountered so few men worth dating in LA, and when I met Too Good, he said, "I'm not looking to play games. I know what I like in a woman, and I see it in you." I felt an incredible sense of anticipation to discover what would unfold with him. It's not that I'd suddenly become that girl looking for a man to put a ring on it. Quite the opposite; I'd suffered too much to earn my freedom to ever want to give it away. I was, however, coming to the conclusion that I was at my best in a loving relationship—not having casual affairs. My experience with the Big One had taught me that. I needed sex. I enjoyed affection. Maybe it was time I gave love another try.

As I listen to the angry voicemail from Too Good To Be True, I realize that in my excitement to get back in the saddle of love, I almost fell for the oldest trap out there: The controlling, overly-possessive guy who's in a hurry to find the genetically perfect wife to carry on his seed and act as his private caretaker; any chick with the basic qualifications will do. I'm beautiful (ensuring cute kids and the ability to get a hard-on), I'm tall (impregnating me would guarantee his offspring extra inches, and they'll need them), I'm stylish (he was a designer so that probably garnered me huge points on his sliding scale), I'm well-spoken (kind of irrelevant to him, but a nice bonus at dinner parties), and I'm great mom material (the sole purpose of my existence, no doubt). Batta-bing-batta-boom, who cares about my actual person or identity? I would just be a means of perpetuating his identity, in the form of "mini-mes," anyway.

My mistake was thinking his single-minded determination was prompted by my fabulous self, not just a general desire to be married and settled. Basically, this kind of guy is the male equivalent of the girl who just wants a husband, and any schmuck with enough cash will fit the bill. I'm not that girl. I don't care how bloody rich he is. I've tons of rich men knocking at my door. I'm not for sale. I'm for free—for the right guy.

The thing is, I want more than wealth. I'm an ambitious girl. I want it all! Respect for my individuality, love for my spirit, and passion for my mind as well as my body. I want the man to know what a treasure he has, and for him to value me as more than an extension of his own ego. If all those things were in play, and I felt the same about him, I'd be willing to consider perpetuating the species with that amazing fellow. Until or unless that glorious day arrives though, I want to be free. Anyone who is going to get angry when he goes a couple of hours without being able to get through to me sounds bloody scary. First of all, he is too damn controlling, and second, he obviously didn't really look at me, or he would have seen I'm as trustworthy as they come.

Lying by No Boundaries's swimming pool, composing the formal rejection letter I will send to Too Good to Be True in my head, I laugh at myself. Okay, so maybe a novel-length letter to end one week of dating is a bit overkill, but what can I say? I'm a bloody writer. I need to clearly express myself. Any guy who actually deserves me will appreciate my propensity to make myself clear with a plethora of words. Until that fabulous man arrives, I will not be Captured, Spread, and Pinned (literally or figuratively). Nope, I'll keep flitting around, dodging nets and being carried aloft on the breeze of life, unfettered and full of magic.

Dinner Menu for the Week

Monday:
Top Ramen
Tap water
1 stale Red Vines licorice stick

Tuesday:
Plain spaghetti noodles
Tap water
1/2 Snickers bar

Wednesday:
Fusilli noodles
1 glass Two Buck Chuck (Charles Shaw Vino)
Handful of airline peanuts

Thursday:
Penne
Tap water
Spoonful of brown sugar melted with butter

Friday:
Steak w/ baked potato and creamed corn
Truffled macaroni and cheese
Chocolate lava cake
2 glasses Bordeaux
1 vodka tonic

Saturday:
Crispy rice, spicy tuna sushi, baked crab hand rolls, and shrimp tempura
Sake
Perrier
Mochi ice cream
Veuve Clicquot
3 mints

Sunday:
Leftover truffled mac and cheese
Tap water
Pack of Smarties

THE DATING DIET

*D*a *na na nah. Da na na-nah. Da da daa daa, da da da da daa!*

The theme song from *Mission Impossible* pulses through my head as I whip my car into the parking lot and survey the surrounding area. Taking a deep breath, I pull off my flip-flops and slide into my four-inch, olive-green heels before exiting the Little Pip. I glance over my shoulder to make sure I'm not being followed as I make my way across the piping-hot pavement to the unassuming building in front of me. The coast looks clear. I open the door and enter the lobby. A cool blast of air rushes across my fevered skin.

I survey the perimeter.

A middle-aged receptionist sits at the front desk filing her nails. "Can I help you?"

Oh shit, I don't want to sign in. There can't be any evidence of my being here. What am I going to do? "Actually, no. I was just..."

And then I hear it. Riiiiiiiing, riiiing!

Saved by the phone! The receptionist presses the phone to her shiny fuchsia-stained lips, and I summon my James Bond stealth and Fred Astaire grace to sneak past her.

Making my way down the hall, my eyes are on the lookout for office number 106. Voilà! I've arrived. I study the door on pins and needles. Am I really going through with this?

I really don't have a choice.

Pulling my shoulders back and courage up, I raise my hand and knock. From the other side of the door, I hear the sound of rustling papers, followed by a squeak of a file cabinet being closed.

"Come in," a hoarse, raspy voice barks from the other side. I don't doubt this man has chain-smoked Marlboro Reds for forty-plus years.

Pulling the door open, I enter the cramped, dusky office space. I've just stepped back in time. Actual filing cabinets line the back of the room, and on the desk there's a Rolodex and a real-life typewriter with paper in it, just waiting to be used. From the walls, black-and-white framed photos of Brando, Marilyn, Rita, and Bing stare down at me. Is that condemnation in their eyes? I can't help but wonder.

The man sitting behind the desk looks like a B-level mafia don. Rounded from years of indulging in too much food and wine, bald as Daddy Warbucks and approaching seventy, he doesn't even bother to rise when I enter.

Pointing to a chair, he barks, "Sit down."

Gingerly, I take a seat on the edge of the chair. In my head, I've mapped the quickest route to the door, and I'm prepared to flee at anytime. It has not escaped my attention that the Don is old, and I have firsthand knowledge of how shady old men with power can be in Hollywood. I know for certain this particular one's shady, because I'm here to do shady business with him.

This Sunday school-raised good girl is on her way to the dark side to dance with the devil, or at the very least, trick the all-powerful Screen Actors Guild.

My decision to take the plunge from moral heights to the gray zone came last week after an incident with my fridge and the ensuing date it inspired. It started out like any other Friday in Tinsel Town, with me gazing into my fridge and pondering how I could turn a pickle, yogurt, and stale tortillas into an appetizing meal. I'm no Martha Stewart, but even a culinary genius couldn't pull that off. Giving up, I grabbed my wallet, dug through it, and discovered... absolutely nothing. I wasn't terribly surprised, as there hadn't been anything in it five minutes ago, but what could I say? Hope sprang eternal. My stomach growled another angry demand for nourishment. It was time to throw in the towel, surrender my self-sufficient pride, and enlist the old backup plan. I picked up my phone and began scrolling through my contacts.

"Hmmm, who will it be?" I said to myself. "I can't ask him, he might get the wrong idea. No, not him either; I can't call two weeks in a row. Not him; I'd rather starve than listen to him drone on about his latest movie for three hours. Oh wait, here we go—we've got a winner, he's perfect." I'd love to see him and catch up. Besides, he's got really great taste in restaurants.

Texting: *Feel like feeding a starving writer tonight?*

I begin another round of the Dating Diet.

Diets are all the rage in Hollywood. Every magazine talks about the latest diet craze the stars are following and how thin Hollywood has become. We hear of the Atkins Diet, the Cabbage Soup Diet, the Raw Food Diet, the Blood Type Diet, the Coconut Diet, and the (you've got to be kidding me) Green Tea Diet. But nobody ever talks about the real diet of Hollywood; the diet that keeps all the not-yet-famous actresses thin. I like to call it the Dating Diet. It's pretty simple, actually. All it requires is an empty bank account, a cute face, and a lot of male friends. Many a would-be actress/artist has survived on it for years.

Here's how it works. You stretch your miniscule resources as thin as you can by living on the cheapest thing you can buy: pasta. Yes, it's true. Top Ramen, spaghetti, macaroni and cheese, and even the fancy fusilli all cost less than one single organic vegetable. Then you offset your pure-carb penny diet with dinner invites from less financially challenged male friends. Here's the chance to devour the best food in LA from the very best restaurants. Of course, this fabulous food is washed down with the finest champagne and followed with a delectable dessert. But even with this sporadic, hearty intake of food, your little body doesn't gain a pound. The ideology behind this highly successful diet is that your poor system is in such a state of perpetual confusion about what it will be given that it simply forgets how to make fat.

Some girls take the Dating Diet to the next level and put out. The hearty physical exercise involved in a sex session burns a ton of calories and can increase the diet's success rate. I, for one, am not that committed to the diet and prefer to choose men who merely want a bait date. I have a lot of male friends who have gotten lucky after being seen with me on their arm. The way I see it, for those guys, it's a win-win situation. But hey, I can't fault the extreme dating dieter—after all, that's dedication. And don't they say a true diet requires dedication?

Beep. Beep.

I grabbed my phone and looked at it.

"Of course, doll. Pick you up in twenty."

I closed the door on my empty refrigerator and dashed for the bathroom to get myself ready. I threw on makeup, a baby-doll dress, and strappy heels in preparation for my date's arrival. I had to do my part of the bait date deal. It is an unwritten rule: you must dress hot. No girl in ratty sweats was going to make other women want a man.

I expected delicious food and drinks from the night. What I did not expect was for my date to decide that this was the night he would take our friendship to a whole new level and change the rules of the game. He'd had recent luck with an extreme dating dieter and decided to give it a shot with me, despite the fact that I'd previously informed him thus:

"It will not happen. Not ever, ever, ever. Not even if hell freezes over. Don't even think about it. I'm merely your bait date. Think of me as an advertisement, not a product."

Obviously my language had been too ambiguous for him.

It wasn't a huge deal. He took the rejection relatively well, but just the attempt was enough to ruin the evening and put me off on hanging out with him again. The experience also painfully drove home the need to find a way to fix my tenuous financial position. Dating for attraction or fun was one thing. Dating as the only thing standing between me and certain starvation was another thing altogether. The Dating Diet had to end.

For months I'd been trying to figure out how to get into the Screen Actors Guild union, also known as SAG, so that I could make one hundred and fifteen dollars a day as an extra instead of a lousy fifty-four. But after this date, I knew it was imperative to my survival in Hollywood.

For those of you who don't know, SAG is not an easy "club" to get into. Unfortunately, it takes a lot more than being an actor to get your access card. The German had explained to me the standard protocol with SAG: There had to be three occasions where a casting director, in their search for the perfect background extras, decided that none of the other millions of union extras fit the background character they needed, except you, so they hired you at union wage. Three pay vouchers indicating you were hired at union wage was your golden ticket to be part of SAG. Once you have those, you could join. Oh, did I mention the part about signing the dotted line in blood, giving SAG your firstborn child, and paying fourteen hundred and six dollars in joining dues?

Despite the rather hefty cost of membership, I was willing to pay. My only problem was that I couldn't get the three union vouchers.

In the beginning I asked myself, "How is this possible? With my dazzling 'it-ness,' my long legs, and my award-winning smile. Surely a girl like me is indispensable background ornamentation for the glamorous movies of Hollywood?" And then I discovered cold, hard reality. In the rest of the world, I might be a pretty darn special little "it-miss," but in Hollywood, I was a dime a dozen. In my wildest dreams back in Oregon, I would never have believed it possible. It was sad but true: for the first time in my life, I was common. How ironic that the thing I'd tried for all those years back in high school to attain was now something

I desperately wanted to avoid. Hollywood is full of Amazonian beauties. Supermodel looks and height are the norm. If I wanted a casting director to insist that I was the only person who could fit the part out of all the already unionized people, I would have had better luck being a midget, bearded, or the four-hundred-pound lady. My type was as prevalent as cockroaches and not as well respected.

Whenever I asked any of the union extras on a job how they got in, they gave me evasive, muddled answers, which basically equated to:

"There is no way in hell we are telling the likes of you!"

It was a secret society, and I didn't know the special handshake.

The German had gotten in through her modeling agency. Apparently my C-level-at-best agency did not have the same kind of connections. I was out of luck.

At least, until last week.

I was working as a non-union extra on the set of a horror film. Covered in fake blood and bruises as the victim of a murderous rampage by a serial killer, I was quite a shabby sight. It was probably my tragic state of appearance that brought out the chivalrous nature of the gentleman from Colorado I sat next to at lunch. But whatever it was, he took pity on me and bequeathed me the insider knowledge I'd been questing for since my arrival in Tinsel Town nine months earlier.

"I got mine the way ninety percent of the people here do," he told me. "I bought them!"

"What? Seriously?" I screamed before lowering my voice to a whisper. We were, after all, lunching with hundreds of SAG members. "I always knew there was some kind of scam involved, but I thought it involved blow jobs. Who did you buy them from?"

"Lots of industry people sell them, but I got mine through this manager out in the Valley. He has some kind of deal with several casting directors, and they split the take."

"How much did it cost?"

"Seventy-five a voucher."

"Wow. Seriously? I wasn't down with a sex trade for them, but I'm willing to buy them if that's what it takes. Will you give me his name and number?"

"Sure," he said, and scribbled something down on a paper napkin. "Just tell him Colorado sent you."

I'd learned the secret handshake. Now I could join the club and actually find a way to survive in this town. It was really happening. The days of Dating Diets for Charity Gaye Finnestad were about to become extinct!

I was nervous but excited when I called the Don that very day on my drive home. He answered the phone with a raspy voice. He sounded straight out of a mobster movie.

"Hi, my name is Charity Gaye Finnestad, and I'm a friend of Colorado's. He was saying..."

Before I could utter another word, the Don cut me off. "Can you come to my office Tuesday morning at ten?"

"Uh, sure. Is that how you normally do it?" I asked.

"Do what? I don't do anything."

Shit, clearly I'm a failure at shady negotiations!

"Um. Uh... I'm sorry," I said. "I thought..."

"Ten o'clock sharp! See you then." (*Click.*)

Okay, that was just weird. What does this guy think? That I'm some undercover SAG agent ferreting out his scam? Well, hell. Maybe he does. I know if I was running a scam like that, I'd be afraid all the time. Or maybe he thinks his lines are tapped. I suppose that's possible, too. Technically he is a criminal. Dear lord, I'm doing a shady deal with a criminal! What have I come to?

The instant I got off the phone, I called the German.

"You won't believe what just happened."

I proceeded to tell her exactly where I would be at ten o'clock Tuesday morning and why I would be there, "just in case." After being delighted that I'd finally found a way to get into the union, she agreed with my caution: "Yep, that's definitely the scene in the movie where the girl disappears. Maybe I should go with you."

"No. No. I can do it myself. I just wanted to make sure someone knows where I'm at. I'm probably being a little paranoid here, but better safe than sorry."

"You're not paranoid. It's the Valley! Crazy shit happens over there."

I laughed. I hadn't even thought of that.

"Don't worry," the German says. "If I don't hear back from you by ten forty-five, I'll put on my trench coat and call the LAPD." My own sexy German Columbo. This was going to be an interesting Tuesday.

Five days later, perched on the edge of my seat in the Don's den of the past, I have to conclude that this is indeed an interesting Tuesday. Since I entered, the Don hasn't stopped regaling me with small talk about the weather, traffic, and the glory days of Hollywood. Not a single mention of SAG vouchers, payoffs, or insider bribes in sight. After fifteen minutes of chitchat, I'm beginning to wonder if this whole thing is a setup. Maybe Colorado wasn't such a gentleman after all. Maybe he sent me into this legit manager's office to pull a joke on me. Maybe he knew this guy was a lonely old dude who would talk my ear off and not help me one iota.

I know I can bring the vouchers up myself, but I'm way too nervous. What if this is a setup? I can see it now: Right when I open my mouth and ask, a SAG cop jumps out of the closet and screams, "Gotcha, cheater. You're going to union hell!" I'll be blackballed for life.

I squirm on the edge of my seat as fifteen minutes turns into thirty. He better hurry—the German is going to bust in the door with the LAPD any second now. Clearly this guy has all the time in the world to chat, and nobody to chat with. But I don't! I need to get out of here and find another way to make money if this is not going to work. And just as I'm about to excuse myself, thwarted in my efforts, he addresses the elephant in the room, halfway through a sentence about Old Blue Eyes.

"Okay, doll, you need union vouchers. I'll get them for you."

"What?"

The subject change was so fast I couldn't keep up. The dumbfounded look on my face caught him by surprise.

"You need vouchers, right? You said Colorado sent you, I assumed…"

Elated!

"Oh yes, yes I do. Thank you. So how does it work?"

"I get you hired on three union jobs, and you pay me two hundred dollars a job. You pay up front in cash. But don't worry, you'll make it back in no time if the shoot has overtime."

Not quite as elated.

"But Colorado said it was seventy-five."

"That was before. Rates change. You still want to do it?"

I didn't really have much choice. It wasn't like I could bargain shop on Amazon for dirty casting directors who had found a way to double their income on the backs of struggling artists. He was the only SAG entryway I knew. The legit way would clearly never work for someone like me.

"Yes. Absolutely yes."

"Okay, get me the cash, and I'll have you on your first job tomorrow."

Tomorrow! Hallelujah! Glory be! I never expected it to happen that fast. Why, at that rate, I could be part of the union in a week.

Wait a minute… I still need to find a fountain pen to fill with blood, have a firstborn child to hand over, and come up with two thousand and six dollars cash. That's an awful lot to accomplish in one day. I feel the need for a nap just thinking about it.

Ah hell, though, this is Hollywood; anything can happen!

I pull out of the parking lot and head for an ATM, speed dialing the German as I go.

"It worked! It worked! SAG, here I come," I shriek into her ear.

"What? What are you talking about?"

"I just met with the Don. He's going to do it."

"Oh, is it Tuesday already?"

Oh lordie, it's a good thing the Don isn't a super-criminal intent on kidnapping young women and offing them, or I'd be a goner. Hell, the trail to my remains would be stone-cold long before the German realized what day of the week it was.

"You seriously need a calendar," I inform her. "Don't worry, I'll buy you one with my SAG money."

"This is great news, Charity."

"I know. I can't believe it's finally happening."

"It's about damn time."

"Tell me about it!"

Exactly thirteen days, seven hours, and eight minutes later, it's official. I'm standing in the SAG office signing the paperwork that will make me a full-fledged member. Sure, I'm technically now a SAG criminal and have two thousand and six dollars in credit card debt to pay off, but I'm going to make that money a lot faster at one hundred and fifteen a day than fifty-four. My days of the Dating Diet are numbered. I can see the light at the end of the tunnel. The feast at the end of the fast. I'm on my way.

Cracked out on kisses [krakt out ȯn **kis**-is]

Medical Definition:

A commonly held, under-diagnosed medical condition where a compulsive dependence on kisses from a specific supplier obliterates all sense of rationality, intelligence, or common sense. Delusions and daydreams are common symptoms among the infected. Patients suffering from this malady (i.e., Charity Gaye Finnestad) can frequently be found kissing frogs in corners, hoping they will turn into princes.

There is no known cure for this condition at this time, but the Institute of Lip Lock has researchers working around the clock in hopes of saving untold masses from the devastating effects of the epidemic, which include, but are not limited to broken hearts, bad marriages, public humiliation, rabies, STDs, and extreme weight fluctuation.

LOVE LENSES

Tears pour in rivers down my face as I sit on a bar stool at the dimly lit, unusually busy Library Bar in West Hollywood. In no time flat, a lake of desolation starts to form on my corduroy skirt. The bartender who had been hanging in my vicinity, flirting with me, hastily retreats to the other side of the bar the minute he notices the extreme weather change.

I can't say I blame him. A woman's tears are kryptonite for most men. They certainly are for my companion: the fellow inducing these tears with the message he's delivering. He looks like he's about to have a heart attack. Beads of sweat cover his brow and he fumbles to hand me napkins, his eyes darting toward the door with every sob that bursts from my trembling lips. I'm pretty sure he's preparing to make a run for it. On some level, I know I'm making a fool of myself. I should pull my shit together, act nonchalant, and not let the Messenger know how devastated his news is making me. He's sure to report my reaction back to the message-sender the minute he leaves, and I'll be without even a shred of self-respect to walk away with. But I can't. Dignity and pride have gone out the window. My heart has been broken into a million pieces and the only viable response is a good old-fashioned Charity meltdown.

I've just been dumped—via proxy!

I honestly can't believe it's happening. It's too ludicrous for words. At first, I thought it was some kind of sick joke, but when the Messenger didn't yell, "Psych!" and start laughing when the tears rolled in, I realized it was the real deal. A breakup, a heart smash, an ending. And not even by the man I've been in the relationship with. Who does something like this? Who sends their best friend to do their dirty work instead of doing it themselves? I'll tell you who: junior high girls, and the gentleman I had the misguided misfortune to fall in love with. The Duck.

When I first met the Duck, I never would have imagined that someday I would be crying my eyes out over him. In fact, the truth is, I don't even remember the first time we met. He was so insignificant to my world that he didn't leave an impression until the second introduction, and then only because he worked really hard at it. We were at a dive bar in Los Feliz, where I was throwing a birthday party for my dear friend, the Duchess. In the spirit of any good dive bar, the Duchess and I were drinking tequila like it was water. I was high on life and my friends.

According to the witnesses, I met all the friends of friends who came to celebrate the Duchess's birthday, including the Duck, but I sure as hell don't remember it. I was too busy dancing on the bar and kissing a total stranger with black hair and green eyes. It wasn't until later in the evening, when Green Eyes asked about my blonde friend who'd been watching me all night, that I even realized the Duck existed.

"Who, that guy? I've never seen him before."

The Duck heard every word I said. Now that I think about it, I bet that was the instant he decided he was damn well going to leave his mark.

Bursting into a fresh round of tears, I wonder why it is that men always want what they can't have until they have it. That's where I screwed up. I should have never let him know he had me.

Anyway, I digress; back to the night I met the Duck. Since his first effort at meeting me had proved a colossal failure, the Duck tried again, only this time with a vengeance. First, he had the Duchess pull me out of a lip-lock with Green Eyes and reintroduce us. Then he pulled out all the stops to get my attention. Puffed up like a peacock, he regaled me with exciting stories of his life as an international man of mystery, and his mad success in the art world. He even went so far as to tell me he was a bestselling author, and when I laughed him off, he got his books out of the trunk of his black Jag to prove it. No joke!

"Who drives around with a trunk full of their books? Do you also have a plane parked nearby so we can jet off to Europe and check out all the galleries you say your art hangs in?"

I teased him. He pressed forward. Working even harder, he expounded on family dinners at the table with Fellini growing up, and helping Sexy Mega Movie Star pick out her wedding ring. My only response to his ever-escalating stories was laughter. He was clearly full of himself. I didn't want to give his oversized ego any more fuel by showing him he had my attention, but I must admit, secretly I was impressed.

Sure he was a braggart, but so was every single man I'd met since I moved to Tinsel Town. I'm pretty convinced that the Frank Sinatra song, "Come Blow Your Horn," is their doctrine creed…

"Make like a Mister Milquetoast and you'll get shut out,

Make like a Mister Meek and you'll get cut out,

Make like a little lamb and wham, you're shorn,

I tell you chum; it's time to come blow your horn!"

The difference between Duck and every other trumpeter in Hollywood was that he might actually have had something to toot about. He certainly wasn't your average bird.

For a girl whose dream was to be a writer, a man with a couple of *New York Times* bestsellers was as close to a god as I'd seen so far. Unlike most girls in LA who go weak in the knees for film guys, I go weak in the knees for literary and artist types. I'll admit there is a possibility that it was the shiny book cover and the smell of ink on paper that made me fall in love, and that it was not his blue eyes, blonde hair, and fuzzy fur-covered body. But the truth is, I came to love everything about that man, including his distinctive duck-like walk, in no time flat. I even loved that he was arrogant enough to write his own *Wikipedia* page. It wasn't narcissism. It was pure genius. The world would see him the way he saw himself. He was wonderful, and even better than that, Mr. Wonderful thought I was wonderful! Can you imagine? It was a drug.

A typical scene in the Duck/Charity Theater of Romance went something like this:

The Duck, the Messenger (the Duck's ever-present sidekick), and I lay poolside at the Beverly Hills Hotel where the Duck lived. ("Commitment" was a four-letter word to him, and he couldn't even find an apartment worth signing a lease for, let alone a house, so he'd been forking out a small fortune for the past six months to remain commitment-free.) Noticing that a handsome Italian lounging on the opposite side of the pool was smoking a highly exotic cigarette, the Duck asked me and the Messenger if we had ever tried one.

"No," we responded.

The Duck then began a thirty minute rant on how perfect the flavor of these fags were when they hit your lips, and how religious the experience of smoking one was. We'd never smoked a cigarette unless we'd had one of these. The Duck specialized in lengthy rants like this about things he loved, me included. It's how he created his own reality and then shared it with others. I found it utterly endearing. I could've lived in his reality forever, but let's face it—I'm more of a girl of action than theory, and he had made me mighty curious about those cigarettes. If nirvana was a flavor, I wanted to taste it.

While the Duck ranted, I got off my lounger, jumped in the pool, and swam toward the Italian's side. The Duck, shocked and appalled that I, who normally hung on his every word, would leave mid-lecture, gazed on in dazed confusion. I could hear his thoughts all the way across the pool.

"What was the world coming to?"

When I reached the far side, I did my best Daryl Hannah exit, water pouring in rivers down my tanned body and tiny black bikini. Without pausing, I approached the Italian. The Duck and the Messenger sat across the pool, jaws agape, watching me. I bent over the beautiful man and flirtatiously asked if I could please bum a cigarette.

The Italian, very happy to have my company, graciously handed me one. I put it in my mouth and asked for a light. He motioned me to lean forward and light it off his. I bent down, my lips four inches from a complete stranger's, and touched the end of my cigarette to his. Sucking in air, I heard the sweet crackling of success. No easy feat for a girl who's a non-smoker. When my chimney was blazing, the Italian offered me a seat next to him. I rejected. Blowing him a theatrical farewell kiss, I jumped in the pool and swam back the length of it, all the while precariously keeping the burning cigarette out of the water. When I reached the Duck, I placed the cigarette in his wide-open mouth as the Italian looked on. I grinned at the Messenger, who started laughing.

"See how ungrateful he is? He hasn't even said thank you."

The Duck recovered from his temporary paralysis and joined in the laughter. Then he spent an hour telling me in minute detail how he was going to remember that image until the end of time, and how I was the coolest thing since sliced bread.

When a successful artist looks at you like you are some exotic creature who dropped from the heavens to be his muse, you feel like an exotic creature who dropped from the heavens to be his muse. For some bizarre reason, everything about me fascinated him. The way I cut my own hair, my orange and white-striped dress, my pink alligator heels, my wacky family stories, my total disregard for all uptight conventions, my uninhibited dancing style, and my intense emotional range were all brought up and analyzed for their utter perfection on a regular basis.

My quirky Duck had a gift for hyper-focusing reality in a way that was flattering to two people: himself and me. Like a gifted lighting expert at a photo shoot who knows how to make all the good things about you look great and the bad things disappear, I was seeing myself in a whole new light. Some might call it delusional. I thought it was marvelous. What can I say? Until I met my Duck, I never realized how truly wonderful I was. Clearly the rest of the world ought to be paying tribute to my fantastic greatness. It was only a matter of time until they did. As long as I had my Duck by my side, we would make our way through life tolerating the plebeian masses until we found other beings as great and glorious as we were. If they even existed. Mr. Sheen had nothing on the Duck and I. We were the true "winners."

It was a wonderful drug!

My new Duck drug entered my life right in the beginning of my "Decoding of a Perfectly Programmed Mind" phase. I'd decided that I was tired of living by the programming I'd received my whole life from the outside world: the church, my parents, my schools, the government, etc. I was going to question everything I'd been taught and toss everything that didn't feel intuitively right with my spirit. Then I was going to build an entire new set of beliefs from the ground up using literature, art, poetry, and science. An epic undertaking, I'll admit, but a necessary one if I was going to find any happiness or meaning in life. On a deep level, I knew that the things I'd been taught were fatally flawed.

At the time I met the Duck, I was attempting to "live in the now," like Eckhart Tolle speaks of in *The Power of Now*. "Attempting" being the operative word! Do you know how colossally hard it is to be present and have no future plans when you fall in love?!

I remember spouting off things on our first date that I truly meant in theory, but later wished I could erase from his mind for all eternity. Genius things like, "Don't worry about the future. Just enjoy the present. We don't need to make plans, we have the now." Etc., etc., etc.

Now my ass! Was I on crack? By week two, I was in love and wanted a future with a capital "F." A mid-century modern home in the hills, blonde furry babies, and dinners with Fellini (or at least his modern counterpart)—but how the hell was I ever going to get that when I'd laid the wrong foundation in the beginning? Our roles seemed set in stone. The Duck signed up for a bohemian who asked for nothing and gave everything in the moment, because that's what I promised him. There wasn't any ambiguity for him; my part was clear. I was to be the dazzling, slightly out-of-reach muse to his troubled, eccentric artist. He liked it that way, and whenever I started to veer from the script, he'd pull back. My "I love yous" were met with stony silence, despite the fact that I was convinced he loved me too. How could he not, if I was the only person on the planet as wonderful as he?

Too late, I realized that my new "live in the now" doctrine had screwed everything up. Clearly this belief system was better in theory than in practice. This whole situation was entirely my fault. Unfortunately, I couldn't call for a do-over and start a different way with the Duck. If I could, who knew how different the outcome might have been. Let's be honest: he was willing to work like crazy for me in the beginning. Maybe if I hadn't demanded so little and given so much, he would have worked even harder and valued me even more, but I'll never know now. One of the sad facts of life is that you can't go back.

I guess my last round of drama with him on the phone last night was just too much for his intrepid Swiss heart to take. I keep forgetting that the Swiss are a bottle-your-feelings culture, not a wear-your-heart-on-your-sleeve one. My emotions might be fascinating as a muse, but as a girlfriend, they were scaring the shit out of him. I hadn't heard from him in days (he was off gallivanting around Europe), so when I finally reached him, my neediness came out with a vengeance. I suppose that's why he sent the Messenger to do his dirty work and end things with me today.

I burst into a fresh round of sobs. (*gulp. choke. gasp.*) Will I ever see him again? I can barely believe that the person who has become so central to my life will no longer be in it. My heart's broken into a million pieces. It's tragic! It's worse than tragic! It's a disaster! What's even worse is that now I will have to look at myself through my eyes instead of his. I was getting so used to being fabulous! I rather liked it. Unfortunately, my eyes tend to be rather judgmental and cruel, like those ugly fluorescent light bulbs in offices that show off all your flaws and even make your good traits look bad. This was just too gruesome to contemplate. (*hiccup... choke.*)

"Okay, well, I really gotta go. Do you need me to help you get home or anything?" the shell-shocked Messenger asks me, a look of trepidation on his face.

"No (*hiccup*), I can get myself home. (*sob*) Thanks for being so understanding. I'm just (new round of sobs)... so sad..."

"Look, Charity, you're better off without him. He messes up everyone's life anyway. Just be grateful you didn't marry him."

What was he talking about? I was far better off with him than without him. Didn't he know about the magic lighting?!

"(*sob*) That's exactly what I wish we had done." (Okay, so maybe I'm being slightly dramatic for poetic license, since I still think marriage is for the birds.)

"You do realize he is delusional and a liar, right?"

Well, I think the liar part might be a bit extreme, but yes, I suppose he might be an eensy, teensy bit delusional.

"I like his delusions. (*sob!*)"

"Stop this nonsense. You are way too good for him. I've no idea how he got a girl like you anyway. I could never figure it out."

And with those words, a blinding light exploded in my head. Maybe the Messenger was right. Maybe I am too good for the Duck. Honestly, I would never treat another person the way he was treating me right now. Sending an emissary to break up? Maybe this was not about rejection, but about the Duck's not being able to live up to what I was bringing to the table. Maybe he was too much of an emotional coward.

The real question was, why did I always elevate the Duck in my mind and belittle myself? Who said I needed to maintain the Protestant original sin, self-immolating cruelty to myself that I'd been raised to practice? Maybe the Duck was a gift from the universe to teach me a lesson about perspective. Maybe I ought to make it a practice to celebrate my strengths and not my weaknesses. I don't need to take self-love to the delusional place of arrogance like the Duck had, where there was no room for self-examination and change, but it wouldn't be a bad idea for me to practice some generosity and kindness toward myself.

After all, I came into this life alone, and I was going to leave it alone, so if my traveling companion the whole way through was going to be me, why couldn't I be a better one?

In that instant, I came to the realization it was time for Charity to fall in love with Charity—not a man. It was time to become my own muse, as well as the artist of my life. It was time I wrote my own script instead of reading the lines handed to me. After all, my life *was* my own creation. Like it or not, I was the star of this show. I was the casting director who chose the players who would have key roles; I was the costume designer who picked the outfits I would wear. I was the director who chose the locations I would be in, I was the screenwriter who crafted the lines I would say, and I was even the actress who said the lines. It was about damn time I quit writing a tragedy and viewed the whole thing in a different light.

It was settled. I was no longer going to borrow someone else's lens to view my life through; I was going to take responsibility for being my own bloody director of photography and choose the lens color myself. From this day forward, there was one lens and one lens alone I was going to use to view my entire life and the world around me.

The name of my new lens: radiant rose.

Purr-ception [pur-**sep**-shən]
adjective
1. Contentment or pleasure (as evidenced by an internal purring) with what one perceives, apprehends, or understands about one's own appearance.
2. The ability to buzz with warmth and kindness toward yourself when you gaze in a looking glass.
3. A healthy vision.

Example: "Her purr-ception of herself, as unique in her own right, was shared by everyone she encountered in life."

MIRROR, MIRROR

"I do not see an overweight, middle-aged woman when I look in the mirror!" she declares.

I turn and look over at Mama Mia, who is visiting me from Oregon for the weekend. She is peering intently into the Little Pip's passenger side visor mirror with a defiant, annoyed sparkle in her pretty green eyes.

I giggle, "So what do you see?"

"I still see a girl who's excited and curious about life."

"That's cool, Mom. You are what you believe you are."

"That's why I hate pictures. They don't show the truth."

Oh, I get it. Laughing, I pull out of the Getty Art Museum and reassure her, "I won't send you the plethora of pictures I've forced you to pose for on this trip." As I weave along Mulholland, listening to her "Oooh" and "Ah" like a child at Disneyland at all of the sights, I can't stop thinking about her statement moments earlier. I think my Mama Mia is onto something.

Here in Tinsel Town, we have the antithesis to Mama Mia's mirror. I don't know what kind of black magic has been done on all of our looking glasses, but I cannot count the number of times I've heard young, slim, pretty, healthy girls complaining, "I'm so fat," "I'm getting old," and "I look like shit" while gazing into our Hollywood mirrors. I'm very familiar with the script. I know the exact words I'm supposed to utter in protest, but I can no longer bring myself to say my lines. Like a defiant actress refusing to play my part, I keep silent. It doesn't matter what I say anyway. It's a waste of breath. They want to hear it, but they won't listen, so why bother.

Sure, every once in a while it's the German or the Duchess uttering those words because they are just having a bad day and need a little reassurance, in which case I rise to the occasion. But most of the time it's Hollywood-ites with warped self-perceptions who are completely unwilling to let go of their negative mindset regardless of what you say.

It's a cult in this town to be obsessed with appearance. Proof that you are a member is your ability to recognize perfection and celebrate your lack thereof. I'm not going to lie. It even got to me. When I first moved here, I was influenced by the not-so-subtle indoctrination of the Perfect Syndrome. Sure, I went through the painful adolescent stage when I hated my skinny body with hip bones that stuck out further than my breasts, and legs that made me ten feet taller than all the boys. I used to get teased that if I stood sideways and stuck out my tongue, I would be a human zipper. Or, the frequently repeated, "Do you have to run around in the shower to get wet?" But ever since surviving that terrible period, I've been pretty content with my appearance. I'm very aware that I'm not the most beautiful woman out there, but I'm pretty cute and I do the best I can with everything I've got. Before Hollywood, that was enough, but once I moved here, it was like being in high school again; anything and everything about me seemed inadequate.

That all changed the day I stood with the German in Koi's bathroom and listened to a beautiful Movie Goddess bitching to her friend about how fat and old she was. As I looked at this legendary specimen of womanhood and heard her ludicrous complaints, my stomach turned. It was like a shroud fell over her and she quit looking so beautiful. I suddenly started seeing her through her eyes. Could it be that when I whined about my flaws I sounded as ridiculous, shallow, and self-absorbed as she did? Could it be that I also planted that ugliness in others' minds, not just my own? That was a terrible thought. Right then and there, I decided that I would stop commenting about my little imperfections. It was amazing. Before long, I even quit thinking about them. Soon I was celebrating them. They make me unique. When people were saying how beautiful I was, I had to agree. I was.

Looking over at my sixty-year-old mom, whose body is far from what it was at its prime but whose eyes still have a decidedly girlish sparkle, I feel a massive rush of gratitude. No doubt having a Mama Mia with a Magic Mirror has affected my perception of my appearance and self-worth my whole life. Screw the fairy tale mirror in *Snow White*. Who wants a cruel reflection that tells you who "the fairest of them all" is, when undoubtedly it is not your smiling mug? That's just mean. I want my mom's special mirror that reveals the wide-eyed girl with the whole world still before her in a sixty-year-old woman. That's what I call a real Magic Mirror!

"Mirror, mirror on the wall, where's the beauty in us all?"

The Little Pip's set list:
1. "Jump" by Girls Aloud
2. "Jump" by Girls Aloud (again)
3. "Jump" by Girls Aloud (again with FEELING!)
4. "Man in the Mirror" by Michael Jackson
5. "Let's Go Crazy" by Prince
6. "Oops, I Did It Again" by Britney Spears
7. "If I Can't Have You" by the Bee Gees
8. "Give Me All Night" by Carly Simon

DITTY LITTLE SECRET

"I have no need of half of anything
No half time, no half of a man's attention
Give me all the earth and sky
And at the same time add a new dimension
Half the truth is of no use
Give it all, give it all to me
I can stand it
I am strong that way
Give me all night
Give me the full moon
And if I can't take the whole of you,
Give it to me ANYWAY, Give me all night…"

belt out the words to my favorite Carly Simon song at the top of my lungs. Complete with a dramatic arm throw. You know, the uninhibited one Maria does in *The Sound of Music* while spinning down the hills singing. There is even a little tear-filled catch in my voice at the end of "anyway," because I'm so full of emotion. My entire body is covered in goose bumps, and I'm truly in a world all by myself. Or so I thought. My little heartrending concert is suddenly invaded by loud honking coming from my left. Turning, I see the car next to me jam-packed with people rolling down their windows, cheering, and laughing. It was one of the few moments in my life when I turned red.

Why I would think singing at the top of my lungs with both windows down was private is beyond me, but somehow I really felt it was. I guess I'm so used to everyone in Hollywood using air conditioning and keeping their windows up that it was a shock to realize someone had been listening the whole time. Not to mention watching my theatrical performance.

Feeling like I was caught with my pants down and my whole heart exposed, I decided to go with it—blowing them theater kisses as the light turned green I peel out of there as fast as the Little Pip could.

I don't know what it is about getting discovered doing one of your secret vices, but the feeling leaves you unbelievably unsettled, on edge, and alive. I felt very alive at that moment. My ditty little secret was out.

Yes it's true; I'm a hardcore car performer. I never do it when someone else is in the car, but anytime I'm alone, I'm putting on a private concert or dance show. I know some people sing in their car, but you don't understand . . . I take it to a whole new level. If the Little Pip had a hidden camera and anyone ever saw what I do in my car, I would never be able to show my face in public again. That's right, I don't just sing: I sob with tears streaming down my face while singing sad love songs, I scream with no cares about pitch or tone while singing dance songs, and I act out every single word of every single song with my entire body.

Picture Cher and Bette Midler mixed together sitting in a seat, clutching one hand to the steering wheel and shifting, and you'll get the idea. Yes, ladies and gentlemen, it's not a pretty sight, but I can't stop myself. I love it. In fact, I would go so far as to say those moments are some of my most beautiful in life. That being said, they weren't moments I ever planned on sharing with anyone else, but here I was unknowingly doing it for an audience of five.

As I drive away with the strangest, exposed, vulnerable, butterfly feeling in my belly, I realize, "Hey, that wasn't so bad after all." Sure, some people would think I was mad as a hatter if they caught my little car show, but clearly there are other people out there who simply get a laugh, a smile, and a bit of joy out of watching me live my uninhibited private moment. Maybe my ditty little secret is not so shameful after all. Maybe none of our secrets are. Maybe they're just the things that keep us from really connecting with others. Maybe if we all told one secret to one person we trusted, we would discover it wasn't so terrible after all, and we would all feel a little more alive, connected, and okay with exactly who we are.

I know I do. Heck, I don't just feel okay; I feel great! I just got bloody applause. Yippy Skippy. Today, the Little Pip. Tomorrow, Broadway.

Holly-hood [hä-lē-**hùd**]
noun

1. A community of people living in or around Los Angeles who work in—or simply dream of working in—the entertainment industry.
2. The coolest cats on planet Earth (or Mars for that matter). Just ask them.
3. The shysters, dreamers, illusionists, creators, visionaries, madmen, geniuses, angels, demons (agents), actresses, strippers, actors, car salesmen, dino-sirs, dolls, fuckables, friends, enemies, sinners (there are no saints), and bigger sinners who make the shows (or dream of making the shows) that shape the entire planet's (including your) perception of reality, whether you want them to or not.
4. The dream factory personnel.

Example: "According to the ex-starlet, 'Being part of the Holly-hood was like being part of a cult that only those who were in it could ever comprehend.'"

THERE GOES THE HOLLY-HOOD

I raise my black-gloved hands in the air and wave them back and forth. I step my sexy Gianmarco Lorenzi boots to the right and to the left. When the last note of the song dies away, I let out a deafening scream with the German and the rest of the spellbound crowd. I'm reveling in every soulful note of John Legend's performance when I feel a tap on my shoulder and turn to see an elderly, chubby, short, bald, gentleman staring up at me through large, thick lenses.

"You are an amazing dancer. I can't stop watching you," he declares.

Flattered I reply, "Why, thank you, sir."

Clearly this fellow is a powerful industry player, or he wouldn't be here tonight. It can't hurt to have "his type" dazzled by my fantastical moving and grooving skills. Next, I'll wow him with my keen mind and tell him I'm a writer. Then he'll convene a series of high-powered meetings Monday morning to turn *A Thin Hold*, a screenplay that I just finished writing about kite surfers for my friend Stunt Girl, into the next hit film. Hallelujah, my Fairy Godfather has finally arrived!

I'm at the *TV Guide* Emmy after party, one of the biggest annual soirees in LA. You can pretty much guarantee everyone here who is not stunningly beautiful, or a recognizable face, is a big-shot industry player. Certainly you can rest assured that the men here who are less than Adonises are industry movers and shakers. Maybe a few hot girls, like the German and I, were invited as eye candy for the rich and famous, but certainly no common male plebeians made it onto the list. Or so I thought.

"So, are you a model?" he asks, eyeing my legs.

"No, sir, I'm a writer."

"Wow, smart and beautiful."

I knew it! Today a party, tomorrow a blockbuster.

"So, what brings you here tonight?" I ask.

"I'm friends with her." He points to a middle-aged woman with a horrendous blonde dye job. "Don't you recognize her?" he asks, as I stare at the woman, perplexed, wondering who the hell she is.

The German, a veritable fountain of pop culture knowledge, glances over in the direction he's indicating and says, "Isn't she one of *The Real Housewives of Orange County?*"

"You betcha," he boasts.

Crash, boom, bang. The tumbling wreckage of the naïve Hollywood Rags to Riches fantasy I still occasionally find myself indulging in, despite the three years' education on the absolute ridiculousness of it. Yes, I still believe in Santa Claus, the Tooth Fairy, and mermaids. So shoot me. It's not my fault I was raised on fairytales and the Underdog That Overcame stories. I saw *Rudy*. I know anyone can make a dream come true. For goodness' sake, I live in the city that perpetuates those myths. It's no wonder that sometimes the delusional idea of overnight success gets to me. Sure, most of the time I'm well aware that Instant Stardom is really the product of years of hard work and dedication. In fact, I've been pushing my proverbial plow and building my overnight dream for year after year with absolutely no recognition. But that is not the real issue here. The real issue is, there goes the Holly-hood.

I hate to say it, but the Holly-hood has hit an all-time low when even the biggest Emmy after party is no longer an exclusive artist and industry event. The glitz and glamour of old Hollywood has been replaced by average Joes and Janes, whose only claims to fame is their eagerness to air their dirty laundry for the whole world to view on a weekly basis. Let's be honest; that's exactly what it is. TV stars are rapidly becoming extinct. Now we put our time and energy into watching common folk like ourselves bicker, bitch, and moan while living petty trivial existences, whose only goals are to have the world's attention for fifteen minutes and win a couple of dollars' prize money. I just don't get it.

Sure, I get why the industry people make these crap shows. They're all capitalist-driven, money-making machines, and we buy the stuff, so they produce it. It is a clear-cut case of supply and demand. Not to mention that it's far cheaper to hire Ma Housewife to play herself than Teri Hatcher, so it's costing them nothing to produce this drivel, and it's bringing in bucketloads of cash. What I don't get, though, is why the public eats it up. I wonder why we no longer demand heroes. Why do we prefer to watch other people's uninspired, unenlightening existences? Is it because we long so much to feel okay about all of our own weaknesses and petty problems that we relate to them? Is it because we no longer want to look up and strive for an ideal, and that we prefer to look down and feel as if we are superior and have arrived?

I long for the days when TV shows were a vision of talented writers, a crew, and a cast who brought to life everyday stories with witty dialogue, beauty, and glamour, or a message about the human condition. Reality is overrated. I experience my own trivial reality every day. Give me something that teaches me something new, inspires me, humors me, or challenges me to greater heights personally. The whole concept of celebrating the lowest common denominator just depresses every fiber in my romantic being. It's so completely lacking in poetry.

Looking at the bleached blonde anti-hero who now has a public platform due to her eagerness to have her five minutes of fame at any cost, I decide, fuck it, if that's the way the tables are turning, then I better make sure I'm part of the common riffraff with a seat at the big kids' table. I can still sneak my elevating agenda into the picture once my name and cute mug are recognized by the world. Oprah did it. What I need to remember is that the journey is one reader at a time. On that note, I smile at the starstruck fellow standing in front of me and agree to pose for a picture and, believe it or not, give him an autograph! Yes, it's true, he wants my John Hancock.

Hey, don't laugh. If he keeps it long enough, it may be worth something one day. I may not be getting there tomorrow (sigh), but this girl's not done fighting, or writing, yet.

Smack Happy [smak **ha**-pe]
noun
1. Individuals who enjoy a nice swat to the derriere before, during, or after lovemaking because of the sensation, excitement, suspense, and vulnerability it creates.
2. Folks who dig a spanking.

Example: "She was such a smack happy little miss that she did exactly as instructed and bent over to take it."

RIGHTNESS OF THE WRONG

The beautiful LA skyline twinkles below us, a glistening treasure box of possibilities. It's a balmy summer night, and I'm sitting on the Professor's deck with him and his date for the night, half a dozen of his closest male friends, and the German. We are here celebrating a successful opening that the Professor had at his gallery downtown. I'm convinced the Professor's house has the most magical views in all of Tinsel Town. I fell in love with them the first time I came to his home ten months ago. Wow. That seems like a lifetime ago. A wave of nostalgia crashes over me, sending tears to my eyes. The German, sensing my weakness, pulls me into the mid-century glass house to grab another glass of wine.

"You okay?" she asks.

"Yes. Just a little sad."

"You're doing the right thing," she reassures me.

"I know."

Tonight is my last night in town for an indefinite amount of time. Tomorrow I leave for Zurich to meet up with my new love, Brown Eyes. Who knows what will happen with him and me, or how long it will be before I come back. I'm excited about the possibilities, but I'm going to miss this town and all the people I love here. Shaking the nostalgia off, I pull myself back into the present. "Let's get out there and celebrate new beginnings," I say to the German.

"There's the Charity I know." She raises her glass. We clink and step back onto the porch.

I head for my seat. When I pass the Professor, he yanks me off my feet and I tumble onto his lap. Wrapping his arms around me, he declares to everyone at the party including his new date, "I love this bitch! And she's leaving me."

Conversation stops. Never in my wildest dreams could I have imagined that someone calling me "bitch" in the same sentence that they declare their love for me for the first time could be acceptable, let alone utter perfection, but it is. It's the most perfect love declaration ever—and it doesn't change a thing. He's still right. We're still wrong for each other.

When I met the Professor ten months ago, we were both recovering from terrible heartbreak. I was getting over the Duck, and he was getting over Crazy Cat, a woman who had kept his attention, but terrorized him. Neither of us were ready to fall in love again. Although we didn't say it, we both secretly knew that, on some level, we were still in love with our exes. Thank god we were smart enough to realize that, in relationships (contrary to popular opinion), two halves do not make a whole. Two wholes do. Neither one of us was whole yet.

That being the case, we decided early on to have a very unconventional relationship. I'll never forget the moment we made the deal. We were laying naked in front of his fireplace overlooking the city, limbs tangled after an evening of earth-shattering sex, when he broached the subject.

"You know we're not quite right for each other."

What? Seriously, now? For a second I thought about braining him with the fire iron. It was so close that I could get him with the first swing. What man tells a woman she's not quite right for him when his scent is covering her body and his cum is buried deep inside her? It was too ridiculous for words. My feminine outrage almost got the better of me and made me take a stance I really didn't believe in. Thank god sanity prevailed before I opened my mouth and made a colossal fool of myself. I started laughing instead.

"Your timing could use a little work, mister!"

The truth was, I fully agreed with him. He was great, but I suspected he was not the Magic Man I'd always imagined myself with since I was a girl. The problem was in the direct connection between my peach-ca and my heart. Normally the guy who occupies real estate in my peach-ca also, by default, takes over real estate in my heart. If he hadn't pulled the brutal truth out of the dark and aired it in the light of day, I most likely would have accidentally constructed fairy castles in the sky about us that we ultimately would not have had the capacity to build together. Thank god for his brutal honesty.

"Okay, you have a point, but where does that leave us?" I inquired.

After a lengthy, alcohol-fueled discussion, we decided that we wanted to be together, but we didn't want being together to block us from the possibility of finding the real deal. That very night, we made a pact that we would have an open, "don't ask, don't tell" policy with each other and enjoy each other until, or unless, the real deal came along. In the event of that occurring, I was to give him a cigar to signify the end of the affair, and if he met someone, he was to give me a pearl. If either of us received that from the other, we would stop the affair immediately and remain dear friends for life.

What grownups we were.

I don't think either one of us expected the affair to go on as long as it did, or be as important as it became. It took on a life of its own. It was wonderful. I'd never felt so free and so connected at the same time. During the week I did exactly what I liked with whom I liked. I was a naughty little miss. I had a fling with an Italian, a moment with an Australian, and a regretted encounter with an Idiot. Normally the Professor and I didn't even call each other during the week. Then Friday afternoons I would head up to his home and play house for the weekend.

I knew he loved long skirts and stockings with garters, so I invested in copious quantities. Walking up the stairs to his front door, my skirt swishing against my legs, I would get wet just thinking about what he would do to me. The truth was, the Professor was the best lover I'd ever had. He was one of those rare men who knew how to disrespect you in the bedroom and treat you with the utmost respect outside of it. He introduced me to a world of pleasures I'd only dreamed existed.

On a typical Friday, I would arrive at his place around four and interrupt him in the middle of working on a design for one of his art pieces. (Did I mention he is a madly successful artist, whose accomplishments far outweigh the Duck's, but whose humility keeps him from ever uttering a word of it? I didn't even grasp the scale of his impact until months after we became involved.) When I'd enter, the air would be full of cigar smoke, as he was trying to quit cigarettes by switching to cigarillos. Brilliant logic! Did I complain? No. I hated the smell of cigarettes, but thanks to the Professor, cigars had become to me what the bell was to Pavlov's dog. I'd get dripping wet the minute I smelled one. The scent of a cigar was wrapped up in erotica.

The Professor would greet me with a kiss at the door and ask me what I would like to drink. While he was pouring the drink, he would tell me to bend over his kitchen table. Then he would walk down the hall and fetch a paddle to spank me with. Who knew how fantastic spankings could be? After enacting exquisite torture on my derriere, he would fuck me from behind, leaving me in a state of incomparable bliss. Then he would zip up his pants, make me a mouthwatering dinner, and dive into a discussion on art, philosophy, or world politics.

I was in Charity heaven!

What made it even better was the depth it began to obtain. We weren't daily fixtures in each other's lives like normal relationships, but we became each other's confidants and support system. One would think a relationship like ours would be surface, all fun and games like my relationship with the Big One was, but it wasn't. It was a safe place from the storms of life.

On many a hard night that winter, I drenched his pillowcase in tears dealing with my fears, frustrations, and lack of progress professionally. I wanted to be a writer, but the book I was writing, *"101 Things a Girl Can Do In High Heels"* (about women who had changed the world because of their femininity, not in spite of it), was an epic undertaking that felt like it would never be completed. Realizing I needed a more immediate way of making money, I'd also drafted a screenplay called *A Thin Hold*. I couldn't get anyone to look at that either.

I was paralyzed; reduced to making a living off my external packaging and not my internal content. At first it was fun. Modeling was better than flipping burgers to pay the bills. But it was starting to take its toll. I was ready for my writings and not just my legs to have their day in the sun. I complained endlessly to the Professor about these things. He was a trooper, offering non-judgmental sympathy and support. He encouraged me to just keep pressing on. I treasured him.

We had met in October, and by summer, I was falling in love. Don't blame me. How could I not? What rational girl wouldn't fall in love with a man who fucks your brains out, inspires your mind, and doesn't freak out at the first sign of a tear deluge? He was perfect. We were perfect. Our relationship might seem odd to others, but it was the happiest I'd ever had.

There was only one problem with the little love fantasy I was living in—I was living in it alone.

One day in June, I arrived at the Professor's house to check an email casting notice my agent had sent me. My phone didn't have reception, so I asked the Professor, who was in the bathroom, if I could check it on his computer. He yelled "yes" through the door. Clearly he had forgotten what page his computer was open to. When I sat down and looked at the screen, what should stare back at me but a message box from Match.com with a string of current correspondence with various women. Things like, *Hey sexy, last Tuesday was great,* flashed in my face. I nearly had a heart attack. Where was that damn fire iron when I needed it? This was definitely a braining offense!

You might ask, "But Charity, what about the Italian, the Australian, and the Idiot?"

That was different. I didn't actively pursue them. They just fell into my lap by chance. Here was evidence he was pursuing women besides me! Seriously, what man in his right mind would want anyone else when he had me? Where was that bloody fire iron?

"But I thought you had an open relationship?"

Duh, but somehow that was only supposed to apply to me. Yes, I know that's called a double standard, but who cares. I don't like the way it feels when it is being done to me. Besides, I quit engaging in extracurricular activities a couple months ago because things had gotten so good with the Professor. Why bother with other men when none of them compared to him anyway?

It was at that moment I realized I had a huge problem. Once again I was trying to change the rules of the game right in the middle of playing it. He was not breaking a single rule or being in the least bit unfair with me. I, on the other hand, had broken them all and fallen in love.

Damn my big heart and vulnerable peach-ca!

Before he came out of the bathroom and found me having my devastating lightbulb moment, I closed the Match.com page and opened my email account. When he came out, I tried to play it normal, but there was no question that I was as needy as I'd ever been. Being the patient man he is, he didn't say a word about my extra clinginess; he just gave me an extra heaping of affection.

The next day, as I headed home, I didn't even make it out of his driveway before the floodgates opened. I pulled over two blocks from his house. I couldn't see the road through the blur of salty tears. I called the German and told her my woes. She wasn't surprised. She'd known all along I was falling in love and there was going to come a day of reckoning. How come our friends can always see our lives in crystal-clear vision, and we always see them in a haze? She provided thirty minutes of reassurance that, "Of course he'll never find someone as great as you! He's an idiot for even trying." (God bless her!) We decided that I would talk to him about our original deal next weekend and see if anything had changed for him like it had for me. That left me a week to figure out what to say.

That next Friday, when I made my way up the stairs to his house, I was on pins and needles. What would he say? Surely by now he'd have changed his mind that we were not quite right for each other. How more right could things get than what we were experiencing? I gave it a 50/50 chance he would agree to take it to the next level. I was pretty sure he loved me too, but I wasn't sure if he ever wanted to commit to a relationship again. Like me, he had been married before and was pretty much over the whole concept. I wasn't looking for marriage, but I was looking for a commitment to some kind of a future together. Even if it was this open free one we had. In short, I wanted to take the cigar and pearl off the table.

Speaking of tables, when I arrived inside his place the Professor instructed me to bend over his. Bliss. I knew what was coming. Okay, this wasn't exactly how I imagined starting the conversation, but hey, it would be the perfect icebreaker. Why didn't I think of that? My, oh my, was I surprised when the Professor threw me a curve ball. Instead of spanking and fucking me like normal, he shoved a small silver dildo in my peach-ca and told me to keep it there. Then he sat me down at the table and started preparing dinner.

Normally something like this would totally shut my brain down and turn my peach-ca on, but I hadn't practiced and obsessed compulsively about what to say all week to let a little thing like sexual servitude games get in the way. If we were going to have dinner, I was going to make dinner conversation.

"So, from your perspective, has anything changed with us?"

Boy, did that throw him for a loop. He had no clue what the hell I was talking about.

"What do you mean?"

"You know, our original deal. Have your feelings about it changed?"

I'm pretty sure that was the exact minute I threw a bucket of ice on his hard on.

Completely unsettled, he queried, "Do you think now is a good time to be talking about this?"

No, I think last week was, but I was too much of a coward then.

"Why not?"

"Charity, don't you think it's a good idea for you to take that thing out of you if we're going to have this conversation?"

I guess domination fantasies and relationship talks don't go hand in hand. Who knew? I pulled the dildo out.

"Okay, what's going on?" he asked.

And with those words, he released a tidal wave. I poured my heart out to him. I told him how I'd loved the arrangement we had at first, but that somewhere along the line, things had changed for me and I'd fallen in love with him. I wanted more. I told him how I thought life was a collection of moments and how the moments we were making together were so beautiful and poetic I didn't honestly think they could be topped in partnership with anyone else. I told him he may not have originally been what I thought I wanted, but in practice he had turned out to be just what I needed. I told him he was the most amazing man I'd ever met. I loved his integrity. I loved his honesty. I loved his humor. I loved his smell. I loved his big way of viewing the world. And I loved every moment I'd ever spent with him. I told him if he was willing to commit to me, I would happily commit to him. I held nothing back.

When I finished, I felt like a huge weight had been lifted off my shoulders and that regardless of how he responded, I would be okay. I wasn't interested in having a relationship built only in my imagination anymore. I wanted the real thing, or nothing at all.

He was blindsided by the whole thing. Why is it men never see it coming? I swear, it's like they're completely oblivious to women's feelings. It's not like any of us are very good at hiding them! I'm one of the worst. Only a blind man could miss the neon heart flashing its message on my sleeve.

Once he recovered from his initial shock, the Professor did his male best to put the toothpaste back in the tube and reestablish our original deal. The problem was, as everyone knows, once the toothpaste has been squeezed out, it can never be put back in.

He said he was perfectly happy with how things were going, why mess with a good thing? He was also still pretty convinced that we were not quite right for each other. He told me it wasn't that anything was wrong with me (blah, blah, blah), "It's just that I need a Condoleezza Rice-type of woman." I was many things, but Condoleezza Rice I was not!

It was at that exact moment in time that I realized I would never be the woman the Professor wanted to build a life with. As heartbreaking as it was, it was better to know it now than years down the road when I'd invested more time and energy and turned my back on other possible candidates. It was time I opened the open relationship back up and allowed my heart to meet someone new. I would still stay with the Professor until that occurred. I loved him dearly and wanted to share every possible moment I could with him, but I was going to force my heart and eyes to open back up to the outside world.

I would go back to playing by the original rules of the game.

As it turned out, the only thing blocking me from meeting someone new had been my love for the Professor. Two weeks after I opened my heart up, I fell head over heels in love with Brown Eyes.

When Stunt Girl called and asked me to accompany her and some Swiss friends flying into LA on a night out on the town, I agreed. The Professor was on a trip, so my weekend was free. Little did I know that Brown Eyes, one of the gentlemen visiting, had seen my picture in a Swiss magazine the week before and made a wish to meet the girl in "the red shoes." Within hours of arriving in town, he pulled up to my house with Stunt Girl to take "her friend" out to dinner. When I walked out, he turned to Stunt Girl in shock and asked, "My god, is that the girl in the red shoes?"

I was!

By week's end, we were madly in love and planning my trip to come see him in Switzerland. The whole thing was pure magic. Here was a man who was excited about exploring a future with me and absolutely thrilled to help me construct fairytale castles in the sky. I knew in life there were no guarantees, but there was a very real possibility that Brown Eyes was my Magic Man. Only time would tell, but it sure was going to be fun finding out. He'd already proven himself to be a fantastic lover. The only really sad part was the knowledge that my time with the Professor had officially come to an end.

After Brown Eyes flew back to Zurich, and before the Professor came back from his trip, I began my bittersweet search for the perfect cigar.

Wouldn't you know it? Being a man, the Professor completely forgot the significance of the Cuban Torpedo I handed him last Saturday night. He was delighted.

"How the hell did you get your hands on one of these?"

Seriously?

"Don't you remember what it means?"

He looked at the cigar and looked at me as realization dawned.

"You found someone."

Gulp. Choke. Sob.

"Yes."

"Does he make you happy?"

Wail. Hiccup.

"Yes!"

"Well then I'm happy for you. Stop crying and get over here."

He enveloped me in a bear hug. Pressed against him, I wept. Unlike me, he struggled to hold it together. I just let it fly.

"Seriously, stop crying. I'm the one who should be crying here. You're leaving me."

We stood there clinging to each other under the stars for an infinite time, until the Professor couldn't take it anymore. His voice was rough from the effort it took to hold back his own tears as he pushed me away and swatted my ass. Hefting the cigar in the air he said, "Well, if I'm losing you, I better damn well enjoy smoking this."

Clipping off the end, he did.

"We may not be right for each other, but I really love you," I said.

"I know," was all he said back.

Now, sitting on his lap in front of our closest friends and his new date a week later, he finally says those three little words I so longed to hear the whole time we were together.

"I love you."

It's funny how life works. It really is all about timing. People may tell you time doesn't mean a thing, but they're dead wrong. Timing's everything. There is such a thing as the right person, wrong time. I've seen it happen before. There is also such a thing as the wrong person, right time.

That's what the Professor and I were.

He's not the one I'm supposed to build a world with. He's not the Magic Man. I won't be skinny dipping in his hot tub, or reading books alongside him on the hammock when I'm old and grey. But I am going to love that man and all the right/wrong moments we shared until the day I die. For a moment in time, being wrong with him was exactly right.

Throwing my arms around him, I say, "I knew it, but thank you for finally saying it. I needed to hear it. And yes, I'm leaving like you always said I would. But you better keep your promise that we'll remain lifetime friends, or I'm coming back for that fire iron… to brain you."

Want a fun way to make extra cash, get in shape, or simply tap into your inner sex goddess? We have the answer you've been waiting for!

Join our weekly pole dancing classes and learn how to become an expert seductress. This is the most fun, unique, and erotic exercise routine you will ever experience. Learn how to master the art of pole dancing in a supportive, non-judgmental environment while liberating your inner sex goddess and getting an incredible workout. You will be amazed at the strength, flexibility, and confidence you will gain. This is a class for the lioness in every woman with packages starting at six hundred dollars for eight two-hour classes. No refunds, and no guarantees. We provide the Pole, Instructions, and Music. You provide the inner slut.

HAPPILY NEVER AFTER

I take in a deep breath and square my shoulders. Adding a lightness I don't feel to my voice, I reply to the caller on the other end of the line, "I'm sorry. I don't care what he said. I'm not a stripper. I'm afraid you will have to look elsewhere for entertainment at your party."

Hitting the hang-up button, I feel steam begin spouting out of the top of my head. Just like in *Looney Tunes* right before the fellow blows his top. I look at the phone and seriously consider smashing it against the wall.

How many people has Brown Eyes reached with this nonsense, and why? Technically speaking, he broke up with me. Why the hell is he on this slander revenge rampage? Isn't slander revenge the territory of the broken, not the breakee? And why is it that people change so radically from doing everything in their power to ensure another person's happiness, to wishing them an agonizing life and slow, painful death, simply because they aren't together anymore?

There were five hot minutes when I truly believed that slandering snake was my soulmate. How could I not? Our romance had all the ingredients of a fairy tale: "The Swiss Prince" who saw a picture of his "Dream Fairy Princess" in a magazine. The "Magical Wish" the Prince made to meet the exotic American Princess. The "Fairy Stunt Girl" who granted his wish by introducing him to the Princess. The "Love at First Sight" that occurred between the Prince and Princess.

The "Prince's Evil Ex" who caused problems and had to be vanquished. And the "Fairytale Land" the Prince swept the Princess off to. (Let's be honest, to an American girl raised on Disney movies, Switzerland, with its cobblestone streets, ancient castles, and tiny villages, was my fantasy world come to life.) Sure, it wasn't Tinsel Town, but what girl couldn't use a bit of both in her life?

I never stood a chance against Brown Eyes. After the Duck and the Professor, encountering a man who was generous with his affection, verbal about his love, and proud to show me off was such a novel experience that all my defenses were obliterated and my heart was his for the taking.

When we met, Brown Eyes was in the middle of what can only be defined as a mid-life crisis. He was sick of his life in Zurich and ready for a cataclysmic change. He'd always dreamed of being a chef, but he'd gone into accounting instead. He'd taken the safe route. He was miserable. Meeting me inspired him. Watching a ballsy girl risk everything to go after her dream to be a writer was like watching his ideal self. He decided that he was going to do the same. He was going to open a restaurant in LA. He said, "I know food. You know LA. We'll do it together." I told him my first priority was my book, but if I could help in any way, I would. I also warned him it was a terribly risky venture. "If money grew on trees in LA, I'd be rich. You'll have to be totally committed and prepared for a real uphill struggle."

He assured me, "I'm not afraid of the gamble."

I said there were two ways to approach anything in Tinsel Town: the start-small-and-grow way (which I recommended), or the swing-for-the-fences-big-spender way (which he chose). He assured me that if it didn't work out, he had a plan.

"If the restaurant's a bust, baby, we sell my boat (housed on the Lake of Zurich), buy a small bed and breakfast in Mexico, and live out our days barefoot on the beach." Idyllic images of him and me making love on the sand, laughing into the night with ex-pat guests, and wrapped in each others' wrinkly, suntanned arms flitted through my mind. He painted castles in the sky; either as the toast of LA or a place to get away—we would be happy and be together. I was in. I took the bait hook, line, and sinker, and plopped my heart on the table.

While we waited for his real estate agent to find the perfect property in West Hollywood for the restaurant, we vagabonded around Europe. That dreadfully charming, unbelievably charismatic man wined, dined, and seduced me through three different countries in three different languages. I'd never been happier. It didn't hurt that he was an amazing lover.

One night in Positano, after cruising the Amalfi Coast on a moped, we sat across from each other in a cafe overlooking the sea, eating delicious Italian pasta and drinking vino. Out of the blue, that naughty man told me to spread my legs under the table. I obeyed. Then he took his butter knife off the table and, using the handle end, he began stroking my peach-ca through my panties. I jumped in shock. He told me to pick up my wine glass and keep talking. I was so turned on I couldn't breathe, let alone make small talk, but I obeyed. We were surrounded by people; families having dinner, couples gazing into each other's eyes. I was trembling with passion. Our handsome Italian waiter came up and asked how our meal was. Without missing a beat, Brown Eyes, a wicked sparkle in his eyes, replied, "Buonissimo."

I burst into a round of giggles, which garnered a strange look from the besotted waiter. Thank god he couldn't see under the tablecloth. When the waiter finally left, Brown Eyes looked me square in the face and commanded, "Come right now."

I did! Silently, surrounded by a crowd and shaking like a leaf, I exploded into a thousand beams of light. All of them hanging on his sexy voice. It was pure sensuality and magic come to life. How much closer to Cinderella can a girl's life get in modern times? I mean, for goodness' sake, the story even started with a pair of red heels. Obviously this was my very own fairytale. I was going to treasure every single second of it. And treasure it I did.

Even more, I treasured him: Brown Eyes, my very own Prince Charming. I loved the way he smelled. I loved the way he tasted. I loved his laugh. I loved the way his eyes crinkled up at the corners when he smiled. I loved his charisma, his charm, his social magic, his cooking, his cock.

All that loving fairytale magic lasted for a good six months. The relationship lasted a year and a half.

By the time a property was located and Brown Eyes made the big move to LA to open the restaurant, things were starting to change. At first it was subtle. A little less laughter and kindness. A little more jealousy and insensitivity. But after a while, actual cruelty started revealing itself. A nagging voice in the back of my mind told me, "Charity, he put his good foot forward at first, and this is the 'real' foot. Watch out."

The problem was, I was too far invested. For some stupid reason, my stubborn heart and vulnerable peach-ca refused to let go of the memory of the magic at the beginning of the relationship. I was in love. Never mind that I was in love with a memory. I kept telling myself it was going to go back to that. I refused to believe I'd purchased a lemon. I made a million excuses for him. He didn't grow up with the love I had. He just didn't know how to trust another person. He would learn. I would teach him. I was big enough to handle the verbal blows. It wouldn't really hurt me. I was strong. On and on the delusion went. I kidded myself into accepting treatment I would never have accepted from anyone else. This was only temporary. This was not who he really was. Any day now, we were going to return to the beauty of the first six months. He was under strain. I needed to give him a break. Cut him some slack. So I did. I cut and I cut and I cut. What I didn't realize was that with every bit of slack I cut him, I shortened my own rope. I became smaller. Less confident. Bruised. Broken. Crushed.

His restaurant struggled in LA. Chasing your dreams wasn't as easy as he thought it would be. When he felt bad, his subconscious goal became to make me feel worse. Instead of lashing out at himself, questioning his own decisions and motives, I took the blows. He ripped apart my life and my choices. If he couldn't have what he wanted, then I wasn't going to either. He made me question everything I was or had ever done. He told me to quit writing. The one thing in life he knew I truly loved. Quit dreaming. Do real estate, accounting, anything but art. His lighting wasn't kind. It wasn't even the fluorescent lights of my demons. This was an interrogation light with no other goal than to crush its victim. The obvious conclusion of that lighting—I was worthless.

It got so bad that one night, I found myself on my knees in front of him, begging him to please tell me one single thing he liked about me or found worthy. He was so damn stubborn and intractable that he wouldn't even throw me a tiny bone. He rolled over and went to sleep. Me now, looking at me then, wants to grab her by the shoulders, shake her, and tell her, "Get off your bloody knees, Charity. That position is only appropriate for sucking cocks and meditating, not for begging for scraps of love from a man incapable of giving it."

What can I say? It's a well-known fact that hindsight is much clearer than tunnel vision! I knelt there on the cold wood floor for another thirty minutes, listening to his peaceful snores while tears poured in rivers out of my soul. I was paralyzed. When I finally found the strength to move, I crawled to the bathroom and slept on the icy tile floor, curled in a ball.

How could I have come to this? After the Duck, I'd sworn never to let a man's perception of me hold such sway. I'd made so much progress in my life. I'd learned so much. I'd grown. How could I have fallen for the oldest trick in the drug dealer playbook: Give the mark unlimited supplies of the love drug until they are completely hooked. Then, when they think they can't live without the stupid shit they'd been totally happy without before—cut off the supply and charge for it! Charity with the big heart, original soul, and poofy red carnations reduced to a sniveling mess—thinking a man deserved more love and compassion than she did.

It had to end!

The only problem was, I didn't have the strength to end it. Being the eternal optimist, I was still struggling to let go of the original dream.

Fortunately, he did the dirty work for me. One of his favorite fighting methods was to threaten to leave me. This was how he would get me to crawl back and apologize for things I hadn't done. Anyone in their right mind would say, "Charity, he is doing you a favor, let him leave! Good riddance."

In fact, several of my friends—the German, the Duchess, the Swiss Miss, and even Stunt Girl—had said just that. Remember, though, I wasn't in my right mind. I was in love.

The last time he tried it, though, I called him on his threat. When he told me, "You apologize, or it is over," I asked him a really important question.

"Do you think we have a future?"

He had two choices. Back down on his threat and say, "Yes." Or stick to it and say, "No." He chose, "The way you are behaving, no!"

My heart shattered into a million pieces. A part of me died. With my last scrap of self-preservation, I told him, "Wrong answer. I'm more than willing to go through the hard times with you if I believe we have a future and that the good times will return. But if I'm going through all this for nothing, and it is not even going to work out, I can't do it anymore. There has to be a light at the end of the tunnel."

He wasn't happy with what I was saying. He was getting concerned that I might actually leave. (Who would want to lose the unlimited supply of love and support I was still dishing out?) I gave him another chance. Every fiber of my being wanted him to fight for me. Even a glimmer of a light would have been enough for me to keep deluding myself and stay.

"So you don't think we have a future?"

Proud as ever he said, "Not the way you're behaving."

That was it. The truth. I couldn't lie to myself anymore. We were done. He'd made his choice. I asked him to please move out of my home. He said he didn't have anywhere to go—which was not strictly true, but I didn't press him. Instead I moved out of my own house and onto the Duchess's couch to give him time to find a place. A week later, when I went back to my place to get some clean clothes and check my computer, I discovered, much to my horror, that several condoms were missing. I was furious! In my house, while I lived on a couch crying my eyes out every night! How had I become so pathetic?

That was it!

I went to the restaurant with tears pouring down my face and screamed, "What kind of man are you? Get the fuck out of my house! I never want to see you again!"

He stuttered excuses and insisted I was overreacting, but that was the final straw. We were really done. He couldn't hurt me anymore, or so I thought.

Now I find out three months later that my former soulmate is telling people I'm a stripper! Where does he come up with this shit? He is not the first case I've heard of a bitter ex retaliating, but he is certainly the most inventive. Is it possible I created this with my wish? After all, I did make the Happily Never After wish when I was crying my eyes out over him after the breakup.

You know the wish I mean. You are lying in bed, brokenhearted and bawling over the fact that your dreams of a Happily Ever After have crumbled before you. You are convinced the guy has made a gruesome mistake in breaking up with you, certain he was your one and only soulmate, and positive you will never feel quite complete without him. That's when you make the wish: "I hope he never gets over me and regrets his stupidity in throwing me away for the rest of his life." Yes, that wish.

Everyone who has ever been dumped has made it. I happen to have made it more than once.

It's a natural wish to make. Simply put, it's a desire to have the connection you shared validated and appreciated even though the person is currently tossing you in the circular file. If they regret it later, it will mean that they finally realized how utterly fantastic you are and how special the connection you shared was. Normal, sure, but is it what we really want? I'm starting to think it may not be such a good wish after all.

Relationships are never easy. Ending them is even harder, but there has to be a way to say good-bye to a white picket fence that doesn't involve a Happily Never After. Wouldn't it be so adult if we could collect the people we love and keep them anyway, despite the fact that we don't make the perfect couple? Sure, the nature of the relationship would have to change. A little time and distance would be required to heal, but ultimately turning all our past loves into present friends would be so beautiful.

You know how they say, "Be careful what you wish for." I would say, "Wish carefully for what you actually want." Apparently, it has a lot of power.

With that thought in mind, I carefully place the phone back in its cradle. I'd better quit reacting to Brown Eyes's attacks with a violent desire to destroy things. We aren't going to move very quickly to friend stage if I take a baseball bat to his car or rip out his eyes. In fact, maybe I better look at this in an altogether different way. Maybe he is communicating with me in the only way his neanderthal brain is capable of at the moment. Maybe he isn't trying to destroy my reputation. Maybe he is concerned about my struggling financial situation and is trying to give me professional advice indirectly. After all, strippers make a hell of a lot more money than struggling writer/models, and I sure could use some cash.

Hey, he may have something here. I'm pretty cute naked and not a bad dancer, if I do say so myself. All I need to do is figure out how to use that pole thing, and disentangle myself from my clothes while dancing. If I could master that, I would have backup plan number two, should my backup plan number one (a college degree) fail. It can't hurt to have a long list of backup plans, can it? After all, life—just like relationships—doesn't come with a guarantee. Maybe I will achieve my dreams of writing success, or maybe I will end up kicking in a backup plan and changing directions, just like I did relationally after we broke up.

Thank you, Brown Eyes, I think I'll tighten up my dance moves. Does anyone out there have a practice stripper pole?

Bottle Service [**bä**-t³l **sɘr**-vɘs]
noun
1. A scam perpetuated in LA and other major cities whereby if you desire to have a surface to rest your derriere upon while at a club or bar, you must agree to purchase two bottles of liquor (priced between three and five hundred dollars apiece) which will buy you a table with a handful of chairs and all the mixers to accompany your outrageously overpriced liquor.
2. In other words, to set your weary ass down even for a brief moment while at a club or bar, you must pay six hundred to a thousand dollars for the privilege.

Example: "The popular Man in Black dropped on average of five grand a week on bottle service to provide his posse of girlfriends respite from teetering around in their four-inch stilettos. Naturally, they adored him for it."

THE WISH TO ERASE

Lights flash, music pounds, and drinks flow. The DJ switches songs. Mad with excitement, we leap up on the booth and start jumping up and down. Clapping our hands, we scream the song at the top of our lungs...

And we don't care about the young folks, talking 'bout the young style...

(Peter, Bjorn, and John)

The whole place is chanting the chorus. Caught up in the excitement, the German and I hug each other and nearly fall off our perch. When the song ends, we tumble onto our booth and pour ourselves another drink.

The German and I are out with the Man in Black, our very own VIP. As usual, he's acquired bottle service and therefore a table for our group for the night. I'm a wuss and cannot stand for more than two hours in four-inch heels without a five-minute reprieve. It's a really good thing we have a friend who can afford a table.

There is only one problem with being one of the fortunate few who get bottle service at a table—it's in the math. When ordering drinks from a waitress, one is generally able to keep a clear count of the quantity of poison consumed. Not to mention the time intervals between delivery of said drink and order placement. However, when one has unlimited access to unlimited quantities, on instant demand, one is in grave peril of serious intoxication.

Being a lightweight, this state arrives relatively quickly for me. Yes, it's true: I look at a drink, and I get drunk. Then there is the sexual factor. I sip a drink, and I get hot. That being said, good-girl status and drinking don't go hand-in-hand. They do make an interesting combination, though.

Two and a half years ago, on June 18th, I was a classic case of this schizophrenic mix. What started out as a harmless Sunday afternoon barbecue and pool party turned into a *Bridget Jones*-esque desperate, single-girl shenanigan that I've yet to live down. My only comfort is that the computer containing the video footage of said shenanigan gave up the ghost, so never again will I be forced to relive my humiliating antics in Technicolor. For once in my life, a computer cooperated with me. God bless that malfunctioning hunk of plastic gizmos.

It was a scorching hot day. The setting: a fabulous pad in Beverly Hills owned by Sex Toy Bob. Yes, that really is his name, derived from the products he's made his fortune selling; and yes, he really does have a stripper pole in his living room. The reason for the party: Sweet B, party girl extraordinaire, was turning twenty-five. The participants: everyone in LA. (Okay, perhaps a slight exaggeration for poetic license, but well... it was close enough.)

Upon arriving at the sex mansion, the German, Stunt Girl, the Duchess, and I stripped down to our bikinis and marked our territory at the pool. White plastic chairs may not be worth much at the store, but lying by the side of a popular pool party, they're an invaluable commodity. After staking our waterside claim, it was time to scope out the food and refreshment situation. Strolling over to the barbecue, I discovered, much to my growling belly's dismay, that nothing was sizzling away. Apparently the food was happening that evening. Who invites people over at noon and doesn't feed them until five? Disheartened, but not defeated, I grabbed a drink. Well, if I couldn't eat, I could always drink. Operating on this foolhardy notion, I proceeded to fill my empty belly with vodka. After about the third drink, the missing food situation seemed completely irrelevant. This was the best party ever! And where did all these good-looking men come from?

That, ladies and gentlemen, is the last thing I remember.

My first recollection after that moment was hugging my toilet for eight hours straight. If it wasn't for my lovely friends filling in the details, and a certain now-destroyed video, I would have never known what a good girl does when she gets smashed... she kisses all the boys, grabs their asses, and proceeds to grind on them.

Yes, it's true. The truly embarrassing footage showed me wriggling around in my bikini in what I can only surmise I thought was a sexy dance, kissing men, and grabbing their asses. Who knew I was a grabber? Certainly not I. Could it be, that when I was doing an imitation of Christina Aguilera's "*Dirrty*" by the hot tub and fell in, smacking my head on the side, that I rattled something lose in my brain? (Also caught on tape: an extra little move Christina should have thought of, to lean in and lick the camera while pumping one's ass up and down.) I can only guess, as I've absolutely no memory of kissing or grabbing, and quite frankly, wish no one else did either.

As the music pulses through me and I take a gulp of my freshly poured drink, a thought occurs to me; I cannot erase fifty people's memories as easily as the computer erased the video, so it might be a good idea to try to remember the wish to erase. Maybe then I can circumvent having anything I wish to erase. Sure, it's bloody fun to have a good buzz going, but there is such a fine line between bloody fun and bloody embarrassing. For me, it's drink number four.

With that thought in mind, I set god only knows what number drink down and reach for water instead. I want this evening to end on a happy note, not in an intimate scene with my toilet or an embarrassing tale of grabbing tomorrow. No more wishes to erase for me. I'll take my memories and moments intact, no edits required.

Wondering if you have a severe case of Tinsel-itis?
Common Signs and Symptoms:

1. Your favorite little black dress is turning gray from excessive washing.
2. Your four-inch party heels are falling apart from wear and tear, while the flip-flops and sneakers in your closet still look brand new.
3. When you flip through *US Weekly*, you can list the items in the goodie bags from 80 percent of the parties covered.
4. The paparazzi have finally realized you are not famous and take a cigarette break when you pass them on the red carpet.
5. Your bed sheets are permanently stained with ink from the club hand stamps you forgot to wash off before going to bed.
6. The stack of memento wristbands you keep in your closet could circle the globe twice if taped together.
7. You no longer have to RSVP when you will attend events—only when you will not, as you are now on the permanent guest list.
8. Every single bartender in all of greater LA knows your drink of choice.

TINSEL-ITIS

I rifle through my closet at an absolute loss for what to wear. I've tons of cute clothes, but the problem is I've been going out so frequently that I've worn everything a million times. I don't want to be seen wearing the same thing over and over again. Maybe I should just give up and go with the unique idea the Professor adopted. Ten years ago, he picked one look; striped pants and a black tee-shirt. He has been wearing it ever since. He never has to think about his clothes. Day, night, formal, informal; he wears the same thing. He's essentially created his own uniform for life. Somehow it works. Unlike the Professor, however, I'm obsessed with clothes. On top of that, my taste changes minute by minute. I would never be able to settle on which outfit would be my trademark. The only other way to solve this problem without excessive shopping (which I can't afford) is to quit going out so often, but that's out of the question. I live in Tinsel Town.

In this city, something is happening every night, every day, three hundred and sixty-five days of the year. Each event, be it large or small, is touted as the "can't miss party of the year." Hordes of us, in fear of missing out on the "can't miss" event, forgo laidback evenings curled up on our couches in sweatpants watching TV to venture out to the seemingly endless round of parties and red carpet happenings. We endure hundreds of boring nights at unexciting parties, with even less exciting people, talking about truly tedious topics, to avoid missing that one magical event. The entertainment news channels cruise our parties, recording those two-second windows when someone actually laughs or says something interesting, and then broadcasts it to the world, making us look like a city of glamorous, happy people.

It's like the awards shows. As a girl back in Oregon, I used to watch the Academy Awards, the Grammys, and the Golden Globes, longing to be part of the action. They looked so alive, brilliant, and magical. Now I know—having your teeth cleaned is often more pleasant than attending award shows.

Take the MTV Movie Awards, for example. From my sofa back in Oregon, this looked like the most exciting event of them all, with hordes of screaming fans, rock and roll celebrities laughing and hanging together, and the funny, irreverent speeches made by the winners. The actual event, though, is quite a different sight. The screaming fans are told when to scream by the Master of Ceremonies, who conducts the show. When they don't scream loudly or excitedly enough, they're admonished and told to do it again. During one show, we had to welcome Tom Cruise to the stage three times before we got it right and the impatient MC was satisfied.

The celebrities don't even participate in the show. They sit in the green rooms sipping champagne until five minutes before their category comes up. Their chairs are filled with young wannabe actors hired for the night to be seat fillers. When the celebs do sit down for their cameo moment, the cameras catch every second of their behinds perched in their seats and manipulate the footage to look like they were there the whole time. The funny, irreverent speeches barely garner a laugh from the tired, bored, harassed masses filling the auditorium. The MC once again threatens the crowd, and the cameras zoom in on the one celeb with the acting ability to pull off humor in their disinterested, annoyed state. We were once even told to do a standing ovation. Can you imagine being told to do something that is supposed to be a natural explosion of excitement and praise? If that wasn't nauseating enough, we were told that it wasn't as enthusiastic as it should be and needed to be redone.

With this kind of disillusioning experience bitch-slapping me in the face with the reality of Hollywood, you would think I would know that I'm probably not missing out on anything, and I should just stay home. But here is the thing—every once in a while, for no apparent reason, it's magic! I don't know if it is the stars coming together in the heavens and here on earth or something else, but when this town has its moment, it is amazing. You go out expecting a night like all the rest, and you are blown away by a lovely surprise. You meet fascinating people, you have lively intelligent conversations with the brilliant minds of our time, you laugh until your cheeks hurt, and you dance until you have to be carried home at dawn. In those sacred, beautiful, mind-expanding moments, you know you are living in the most glamorous, cutting-edge city on earth. You know that under all the bullshit and posturing, something special and powerful really is happening here, and you are part of it. You would trade a lifetime of comfortable, ordinary, uninspiring parties in a small, safe hometown for one night like that.

So when you live here, despite the exhausting, boring, tediousness of the never-ending social schedule, you keep showing up. You burn your candle at both ends, working hard during the day and going out every night. You try to guess which events to go to, and you never slow down. When you go out of town for a vacation, you quickly start to feel like you are missing something. You desperately want to be gone from Hollywood and take a break in the real world, but you are filled with the sense that somehow you are being left out of the coolest club in the world. If you move away to escape, you discover this town is a drug, and you are the junkie who quit. You hate the drug. You hate how it consumed your life, but you can't help but remember the good old days, and you know nothing you have experienced since has compared. So you develop a love/hate relationship with it, and burn to return just as much as you yearn to be free.

I know. I've seen it over and over again. I like to think that I'm fireproof; that I'm in the flames, but not burning. Maybe I am. Maybe I'm the one grounded soul who can navigate this town and come out unharmed. Or maybe I'm an addict in denial. Maybe I should just face it. Maybe I have a severe case of tinsel-itis.

Either way, I'm not missing this party tonight. It could be the one. The German will be here any minute. I need to find a bloody outfit to wear. Enough daydreaming; the clock's ticking. It's time to get creative. Okay, if I wear leg warmers over my strappy green heels and throw a ton of pearls over my 1970s micro dress, maybe it will look different. Bingo. That's it. I gotta go.

It's time to jump back into the furnace.

Dino-sir [**dī**-no-sər]

noun

1. An elderly breed of man found in the greater Los Angeles area known for their ability to have one foot in the grave, one on the red carpet, and a prepubescent girl dangling from their arm.
2. Formerly powerful men who now live off of the legend of their glory days and date women young enough to be their granddaughters.
3. Also known as sugar daddies.

Example: "Good thing that dino-sir has two twenty-year-old blondes on each arm—otherwise, he'd need a walker."

DINO-SIRS AND DOLLS

Music blares. The hippest of the cool cats mingle around two Learjets that sport the *Chanel* logo. Journalists shoot pictures of Claudia Schiffer and Karl Lagerfeld posing on the jet ramps. Moments earlier, the jet's arrival was the kickoff for one of the hottest fashion shows ever to grace LA's western shores. Coco would have been proud.

It's the launch party for *Chanel's* new summer line in Santa Monica. Hollywood is out with a vengeance. I stand outside among the crowd of smokers waiting for my friend Swiss Miss, journalist extraordinaire and surrogate big sister, to return from stashing our goodie bags in the car. Bored, I begin chatting with the cute blonde model next to me, comparing jobs we've booked and places we've worked. She starts complaining about Paris. I tell her I never worked there, but when I visited ten years ago right after college, I loved it.

"How old are you anyway?" She asks.

When I say the magic number, thirty-one, her jaw drops. "Wow, you look great for your age."

Something inside of me explodes with shock. For my age?! Is she serious? I'm still a puppy. Gluing a fake smile on my face, I say, "Thanks," as I grab a glass of champagne from the passing waiter and toss it down like water.

"For your age" has to be the cruelest insult I've ever heard in my life! I know people mean well with it, but what they're essentially saying is,

"For a young woman, you look like shit, but for the old bat you are, you don't look half-bad."

I cringe. I can't believe I've been moved into the "for your age" category. For Christ's sake, I haven't even cut my baby teeth on life. Quite frankly, if you ask me, I don't look one day older than Little Miss Chain Smoker who just raped my youthful self-image.

As I slink away to get some fresh air in my lungs, I have a cruel thought: "Keep puffing, Little Missy. That nasty habit is going to make you look ten years older than me at thirty-one." Okay, so maybe it's not fair to wish wrinkles and age spots on a cute little eighteen-year-old who means well, but dear god, I'm still reeling from her blow. The scary news is, this is just the beginning. Ageism, a terrible disease of our time, is rampant in Hollywood—the land of Dino-sirs and Dolls.

Yep, it's a fact; older women here are damn near an extinct species. I see plenty of old geezers around, but never a granny in sight. Dino-sir men are always accompanied by twenty-something blonde girlfriends to the parties and events. It's not just a stereotype; it's true. I've often wondered what happens to the older women. Do they take them out back and shoot them, or are they simply put out to pasture in another city? Maybe the women choose to leave in mass exodus for places where they can be treated with some level of dignity and respect. All I know is they aren't in sight, and I can't blame them. Hollywood definitely doesn't appear to be the place to find happiness with someone at a ripe old age.

The trade-in and trade-up rate is extremely high for relationships in this town. Oftentimes when men upgrade, they go for a newer, though not necessarily better, model—literally and figuratively. Look at the King of Porn. At eighty-five, he is considering having children with a girl who could not only be his daughter, she could quite easily be his great-granddaughter. It's mind-boggling. These guys aren't just father figures; they're bloody grandfather figures.

Don't get me wrong, I'm not an ageist. I believe love is love, and people should be allowed to love whomever they want. Age is irrelevant. Actually, I myself am almost always attracted to men who are several years older than I am. What seems strange to me is that in Hollywood, nobody seems to love the older women.

I hope I'm wrong. I hope the older women are just happily at home knitting scarves for their grandkids or running TV empires with their doting husbands, but if that's the case, how come I never see them? Not at premieres, not at parties, not at dinners, not at the restaurants, not at the grocery store, nowhere. I see tons of male Dino-sirs parading around with their Dolls, but not a Matriarch in sight.

It actually makes me worried. I love this city and the life I'm building here, but will I have to leave one day just because I'm getting older, and older women are not allowed? Fuck, it's completely understandable why women chop apart their precious flesh to try and look like the doll they used to be if people quit loving them because they're older. I wouldn't want people to quit loving me or inviting me to the party just because I have a few miles under my belt. I want to be ninety, wrinkled as a prune, and still shaking it up on the dance floor. I've seen it in Italy, France, and even little old Bend, Oregon, but I've never seen it here. Sad to think. What happens if I build a life, friends, a world here, and just about the time I should be able to start relaxing and enjoying it, I have to leave and start all over somewhere else because I'm not a Doll anymore?

Oh god, this line of thought is so depressing I could just jump in my car, bust on over to the Santa Monica pier, and take a flying leap off the end into legend status. Yep, dying young and beautiful is a sure way to achieve legend status. Oops, I forgot; first I have to do something public and legendary. Grrrr. Well, I guess I'm just going to have to grow old gracefully while working on my great life achievement. Maybe by the time I'm old, we will have gotten our heads out of our asses here in Hollywood, and female age will not be a crime. Hey, maybe I should work on that. Changing age phobia would certainly be a legendary accomplishment.

Pondering the enormous task I'm considering taking on in my strappy little heels, I'm happy to see Swiss Miss return, goodie bag-free and ready to boogie. As I look at this sexy woman, who has several years on me but doesn't look a day over beautiful, I think, "She looks great!" Not for her age. She just looks great!

Decision made, I will never screw up a compliment again by adding that last stupid line. From now on, if I see a beautiful woman, regardless of age, I will just tell her she's beautiful. And also, as long as I feel young and beautiful, I am. Nobody else, and no number on my driver's license, tells me whether I look good or not. I decide that for myself. Wow, two great new life philosophies established in less than five minutes without even breaking a sweat. Not bad!

Speaking of breaking a sweat, I think it's time to take my Doll ass out onto the dance floor with Swiss Miss and shake it. Life is short, and as long as I'm a Doll, I'm going to enjoy all the perks that go with it, including gobs of attention from handsome men. Oddly enough, this particular party is crawling with them; not typical in LA. This is going to be fun.

Whooo-hooo! Two dancing Dolls, coming right up.

Trade-Up Syndrome [**trād**-əp **sin**-drōm]

Medical Definition:

An acute mental illness suffered by a vast number of the population of Tinsel Town that cripples the individual's natural judgment about the value of friendship, propelling them to see friends as stepping-stones rather than loved ones.

A person suffering from this illness will casually dispose of one friend for another—operating under the belief that the new one can help advance them further (be it in career, money, social contacts, or whatever) than the original one. Patients suffering from this malady have no ability to comprehend the saying, "Make new friends, but keep the old. One is silver and the other gold."

PAPER PLATE PEOPLE

I'm lying in bed, curled up in a ball, licking my wounds. Well, actually, I haven't even started licking yet; I'm still crying and howling over them. Hopefully I'll soon move on to the licking part, and shortly after that, I'll drift off to escape sleep.

Okay, maybe I'm being a little dramatic, but the terrible side of Hollywood has reared its ugly head, and this time, I'm its victim. That's right—disposable friendship has struck, and I've been tossed in the circular file. I didn't see this one coming. It blindsided me. Living here four years, I should be more prepared for this kind of thing, but being the eternal optimist, I chose to live in trusting ignorance. That was my mistake, and now I will pay for it. I'm afraid that this time, the price is quite high. I forgot lesson number one in Hollywood: Everyone and everything is disposable. Just like the movie sets that are quickly built and torn down the minute they've outlived their usefulness, friendships are rapidly formed and thrown away just as fast.

Everything in this town feels temporary. Part of the problem is the nomadic nature of this city. With so many people arriving every day, chasing the dream of being a superstar, the city is constantly flooded with new faces. I once read that 90 percent of new transplants leave in the first year. Top that off with the huge number of people traveling to location shoots, the obscene hours, and the grueling lifestyle of the film industry, and you have a city in a state of constant change and upheaval.

With all of this population turnover, Hollywood produces people who excel at adapting. They become truly casual about letting go and moving on. Be it locations, jobs, relationships, or friendships, they say "hello" and "good-bye" with equal ease. The positive side of this mentality is a generosity and openness to newcomers. The drawback is the user attitude that builds up that declares: When you are no longer of service to me, you can be replaced. The truth is that you can and will be replaced many times over in Hollywood. Very few people have the desire or determination to go the distance in friendships or relationships.

Many people think of Hollywood as a surface town. Wherever I go in the world, I hear this said about my city. I would have to disagree with that analysis. The relationships between people go deep very quickly, maybe too quickly. The kind of people who live here are often artists, dreamers, and gamblers. They're by nature unafraid of risk. They take the plunge and go all the way in relationships. There is nothing surface about them. The nature of human contact is more deep sea diving without the proper equipment or a trustworthy partner than shallow water snorkeling. No, the problem is not a lack of depth; it's a lack of longevity. Commitment is a four-letter word to many of the Hollywood crowd. They're just as fearless about leaving a relationship to look for another as they were about starting it in the first place. As soon as the object of their love, friendship, or desire has given everything they have, they decide that they need more and move on to look for it.

Time and again I've seen it happen. This city is compiled of relationship nomads constantly in search of the next best thing. I've personally been thrown away by boyfriends with this sickness, but this is my first time with a trusted girlfriend. I thought I was a better judge of character. I thought she was the real thing; a friend for life. For the last four years, the Duchess and I've shared tears, laughter, and companionship. We've poured out our hearts and dreams to each other. We've been inseparable. Other than the German, she was my closest friend. A couple months ago, Brown Eyes and I broke up. Shortly after that, I quit hearing from her as frequently, then . . . nothing. No response to my calls, texts, emails, notes on her door, etc. There was no fight, no problems, no falling out. Just a disappearing act that baffles my mind and tears out my heart. She didn't even have the courage to say good-bye. She just vanished. Then today, I found out why.

It was a classic case of the trade-up syndrome. It turns out the Duchess has now become close friends with Brown Eyes, a man who she supposedly couldn't stand. A man she insisted vehemently I leave. The same man she has, for some bizarre reason, decided will be of more use to her than I could be in her quest to become an actress.

I wish I could tell her: he won't bring you chicken soup when you are sick. He won't buy you groceries when you are broke. He won't be a shoulder to cry on when you break up with your boyfriend. He won't give you pep talks every time you feel you have hit the end of your rope. He won't cry with you and for you. he won't love you like I do. And he certainly won't be a lifetime friend. What he will do is use you as long as he can, and the minute you are no longer of service to him, he will dispose of you, just like you disposed of me.

But, of course, I won't. No, I will finish my well-deserved cry, pass out from exhaustion, and tomorrow when I wake, I will put on my favorite pair of heels and jump right back into the game. Just like the rest, I will be fearless, fast, and open, but unlike most of them, I'm looking for something to last. I am, in Hollywood, the true exception, a person who views friendships as fine collectible china, and not paper plate people.

The Hollywood Fuckable Girl Price List:

Hand Job:
Recipient Requirements:
1. Was once seen hanging out with a casting director.
2. Sat next to B-level actor or reality show participant at Hemingways.

Fuckable Girl's Return on Investment:
    Hoping for possible introduction to either #1 or #2 above, following services rendered.

Blow Job:
Recipient Requirements:
1. Has a snapshot on his iPhone with his arm around DiCaprio.
2. Was once photographed on the red carpet shaking hands with a working producer.

Fuckable Girl's Return on Investment:
    Hoping for a possible introduction to #1 or #2 above, following services rendered.

A Fuck:
Recipient Requirements:
1. Actually has the phone number of a CAA or William Morris agent in his phone.
2. Can get a table at the Tower Bar, or outdoors at Chateau Marmont.

Fuckable Girl's Return on Investment:
    Hoping for multiple introductions to follow services rendered.

DO A BODY GOOD

I'm coming out of my skin with excitement. In a couple of minutes, my whole life could change. I'm driving into the Hollywood Hills on my way to meet with a powerful producer—The Big Wig; the first person who has ever asked to see my screenplay. I can't believe it. Over the years, I've sent hundreds of copies to agents, managers, and production houses, but they always come back unopened with the hostile word, "Unsolicited" scrawled across the envelope. They may as well just slap me across the face.

Solicited!

I hate that word. Honestly, the only time you ever even hear it is in regards to hookers. You know what I mean: "Congressman Right Wing So-and-So was caught soliciting a Cute Streetwalker, at such-and-such downtown hotel, using federal funds." There is a public outcry, and everyone freaks out that he would dare to solicit the beautiful but lost girl. All I can think is, seriously, a common whore can get solicited to suck a cock, but I can't solicit a reading after pouring blood, sweat, and tears into creating a script? Where is the justice in the world? You tell me how I'm supposed to get solicited if no one besides my college professors has ever even seen my writing? Solicitation is a horrid catch-22, and I'm the one caught in its un-licit-y grip.

No longer! Now all that's changed. A powerful player has solicited a look at my script, and I'm on my way to his house to give it to him. I've finally hit the big time. It doesn't even feel real.

It all started two days ago on the set of a major film production. I was filling in for a friend of mine's assistant, who was sick. I needed the work, and he needed an extra set of hands. I had no idea what I was signing up for. All I knew was he promised me four hundred dollars for two days of work. I was in.

When I arrived on the set, I found out my friend was the art director. Essentially, he's responsible for all visual aspects of the set besides costumes. Since the male members of the crew weren't confident enough to trust me with the handsaw used to actually build the set (despite my insistence that I worked in my dad's shop and knew how to use one), my job for the day involved school-kid-type craft projects. I cut out Styrofoam forms of people and spray-painted them black. I glued glitter onto oversized flowers. I painted lightbulbs red. It was great. I was being paid to do arts and crafts. On top of that, I was having great fun joking around with my fellow crew members, a cast of rowdy men who reminded me of my best buds in high school. They teased the life out of me, and I fake reacted. I grew up with brothers; I know males torment the living crap out of you when they like you. Clearly they loved me. I was in heaven, and I was getting paid to be there.

Just when I thought it couldn't get any better, lunch break was called. This time, I was allowed to eat with the big kids at the yummy hot meals cart. I felt like visiting royalty. As I sat there munching away on noodles Alfredo and a Greek salad, who should sit down right next to me but The Big Wig—the man behind the movie, the producer.

Clearly here was a tastemaker, and my "it-ness" had finally been recognized in all its glory for what it was.

We chatted about every subject under the sun until right before lunch ended, and I finally got up the courage to mention my screenplay. He was thrilled.

"You're a writer, seriously? That's great. I'd love to see your stuff."

I swear that at that exact moment, the heavens opened and I heard a choir of angels singing the Hallelujah chorus. I was solicited! Someone actually wanted to see my work. I nearly had an out-of-body experience when he handed me his business card and said, "Drop me a line and we'll set up a time."

It was all I could do not to tackle him in a bear hug and break into the Yippy Skippy dance. Instead, I managed a calm recital of my standard line regarding my email address; "When you get an email from Charity Gaye Finnestad, and it goes to your spam file, please don't delete it—it's not porn. My parents actually had the audacity to name me that."

To which he laughed and said, "I'll look forward to it, Miss Charity Gaye Finnestad."

That was then. This is now.

I approach the gate at the end of his driveway and lean in to push the intercom button. The gate swings open. I pull up to a view that may even be better than the Professor's. The Big Wig's house perches on the peak of a hill with three-hundred-and-sixty-degree views stretching from downtown to the ocean. The house itself is a beautiful Spanish-style, U-shaped casa formed around a center courtyard with a fountain.

As I approach, the front door swings open and The Big Wig greets me with a, "Welcome to my humble abode."

Humble my ass! This place screams wealth and power. As I walk in the doors, I'm met with the surprising sight of dozens of candles twinkling around the living space. A sense of foreboding assails me. Last time I checked, candles were not standard protocol for a professional meeting. They were more on the romantic side of life. Surely The Big Wig doesn't have designs on me? How could he? He's a hundred years old, and I'm just barely thirty-one! It should be obvious I'm not the Dino-sir dating type; I don't have fake boobs and a blonde dye job. What is he thinking?

Calm down, Charity, you're overreacting. He probably just doesn't have many visitors and likes to show off his house at its best when he does. Yes, that is the answer. He is a lonely old man happy to show off his beautiful home. Relax! Quit panicking, start talking.

"Wow, this place is beautiful. A true testament to your hard work and talent."

Lord, I sounded like a kiss ass. On second thought, stop talking until you relax.

"Would you like to look around?" he asked.

Around? Hell, no, I didn't want to look around! One of those rooms had to be a bedroom. I was starting to feel decidedly uncomfortable being in his personal space. Those candles were giving me the willies. I should have asked to meet at a coffee shop. It never occurred to me that he might be crazy enough to think he would have a chance with someone my age. Surely he doesn't think that. Has he looked at the birth date on his driver's license lately?

"Actually, I don't have a whole lot of time. I was really hoping I could drop off the script and then after you've had a chance to read it, we could get together and talk about it."

"Oh, you have a boyfriend waiting for you somewhere?"

Boyfriend? What? Is he serious? A hundred-year-old man asking me if I have a boyfriend? This is getting creepy. Wait, yes, boyfriend. That was it! If I had an imaginary boyfriend he would have to dismiss any weird ideas he was harboring about me.

"Yes, and I promised I wouldn't be long. He's a little jealous, so if I could just give you this and…"

I extend the script to him. He takes it.

"Text him and tell him you'll be late. I like to read a writer's work with them sitting next to me, so if I have questions they can be cleared up. I find it removes any room for confusion and is a very effective way of determining whether I can work with someone. Let's give this a read."

He turns and walks toward the living area as if expecting me to follow. It looks like I'm not going anywhere. If he is telling the truth, and this is just his process of working, I can't risk offending him. Guess I better fake text my fake boyfriend, *I'm going to be late*. The German is going to wonder what the hell my text is all about, as we had no plans of meeting tonight.

The Big Wig settles onto a long overstuffed couch and motions for me to take a seat beside him. I sit perched on the very edge as far away as I can, leaving about three feet between us. The Big Wig reaches for a bottle of red wine decanting on the coffee table and two glasses sitting next to it.

"Let me guess, part of the process?" I ask.

"Exactly." He smiles.

Wine . . . seriously? Does he think I was born yesterday? Looking at his sun-spotted hands and saggy jowl, I have to admit that from his advanced years, I might look rather fresh out of the womb. As much as I enjoy good Bordeaux, there is no way I'm drinking. I need all my senses on alert just in case he is a perv. What if he drugged the drink? After all, this house is way up in the hills, a long way from anyone. No one will hear me if I scream. He's famous. I'm not. Polanski got away with it, why wouldn't he? This is Hollywood; the rich and famous can murder their wives, pretend the gloves don't fit, and get away with it. I'm in serious danger! Run! Charity run!

Just as I'm about to grab my bag and dash from the house like the hounds of hell are chasing me, I look up and notice he is innocently engrossed in my script. Geez, Charity, there you go again. Just relax. You've come to that blurry line between common sense intuition and total paranoia, and you've taken a dive off the crazy board. He's one of the good guys, remember? A harmless, elderly man who has a lot of power in this town and happens to be interested in your script. Look, he's reading it. Relax. This is all good.

Watching him read and viscerally respond to the writing with laughs, head shakes, and the like, I start to get that magical feeling of butterflies taking over my body. I think he's enjoying it! This is good. Very good. He asks me a few questions as he reads, and I explain my intent. I'm glad I stayed. I see what he means about having the writer present. It really does help with the process. What an amazing night! I can't believe this is happening.

Feeling my confidence in the situation return, I reach for the ignored glass of wine and take a sip. Wow, that is yummy. I take another sip. In no time flat, the glass is empty. He pauses reading and fills it up again. I look at it longingly, but decide not to drink anymore. I'm a little lightheaded already from nerves.

He continues reading, and I wait. Time has never gone so slow. I'm on pins and needles. When will he get to the end? Is my whole life about to change? Hurry! Hurry! I can't take this anymore.

After an eternity, he sets the script down and looks up at me. I feel like my heart is going to explode right out of my chest. My hands are sweating. My legs are trembling. So much hangs on this. He studies me with his head tilted to the side. His face is expressionless. Time comes to a grinding halt. Speak, for Christ's sake! Speak! Just as I'm about to die of anticipation, he opens his mouth.

"Not bad. Not bad at all, for a first effort. Sure, it's raw and can use some refining by skilled hands, but there is no question you have an original voice. I see potential."

I can't control myself. I leap up and do the Yippy Skippy right there in front of one of the most powerful producers in Hollywood in his glorious mansion in the sky.

He starts laughing. "You're really something else, kid. So alive. I knew I liked you."

My cheeks hurt from grinning.

Indicating for me to sit back down, he starts talking. "Let me tell you a little bit about how this town works. You've got something here, no question about it, but that doesn't mean it will ever see the light of day. There's a lot of equally talented writers in this town who can't even get their foot in the door."

"I know! I know!" I shout. "I've literally sent out hundreds of submissions to agencies, managers, and production houses and the only response I've ever gotten was 'Unsolicited!' You're the first person ever to read it!"

"Exactly. I'm your best chance at getting this made."

"I can't believe my luck in meeting you. This is a dream come true."

"I'm glad you see the importance of my role here."

"Oh yes, absolutely! I'll give you all the credit when I tell Matt, and Al on the *Today Show* how this came about."

"I have a little more immediate way you can show me your gratitude."

With that he reaches over and places his hand on my knee.

BOOM! BANG! BAM! My moment of elation comes crashing back to earth and shatters on the floor at my feet. I look at his hand on my knee with a sense of existential detachment. I feel like all the color, smell, and beauty has vanished from the earth, and there is only darkness, decay, and wrinkly groping hands. I'm bitch-slapped by the fall from such heights to such depths. I want to bawl. I won't give the bastard the satisfaction.

If he is going to pull this sneaky conniving shit on me, then I'm going to make him look at it directly in the light of truth. No trickery, false flattery, and unsaid expectations.

"Are you honestly implying if I prostitute myself to you, you will make my movie?"

"No need to be so crass about it darling, that's just the way the world works. A little sugar goes a long way."

"Let me get this straight. If I give you a little sugar, you will make my movie? Am I hearing you correctly?"

"It's not quite that straightforward. There are a lot of people and a lot of money involved in making a film. I can't guarantee it will be made, but I can certainly get it in front of the right people if I have the motivation."

He tries to slide his hand up my leg. I slap it off.

"And the fact that it's a good script is not enough motivation?" I ask. Undeterred.

"You make it worth my while, I'll make it worth yours."

Standing to go, I grab my script out of his hand.

"I see, so that's what all this was about. You have no interest in soliciting my script. You want to solicit my body. Well, guess what, *that* is not for sale!" I wave the script in the air. "This is!"

On that note, I dash toward the front door. As I yank it open, he delivers one parting shot. "Look, if you change your mind, you know where I live."

He really thinks I may still call him?! Turning around, I explode. "That will happen when hell freezes over. You've got a lot of nerve trying to use my dream as a weapon against me. You're nothing but a deceitful, creepy old man."

WHOOSH! CRACK! HISS! The fire from the burning bridge I'm leaving behind nearly singes my soul. I slam the door and run toward my car. I need to get out of here yesterday.

As I drive down the road of broken dreams toward the land of reality check, I keep asking myself, why did he pull that on me? What makes him think he can get away with that bullshit? I'm working myself into a frenzy.

Then it hits me. He tried it, because it works.

I flash back to a conversation I overheard at the Coffee Bean and Tea Leaf on Sunset and Laurel Canyon earlier in the week. The participants, a cute little brunette actress and her rather jaded-looking blonde friend were unapologetic about their treatment of sex as a tradable commodity. The cute little brunette informed her friend, "I couldn't hold him off anymore. I had to blow him. He can help my acting career."

"What does he do?" asked the blonde.

"Well, he's friends with So and So."

"Really? Well, of course you had no choice."

No choice? Well, what do you know? It actually does happen! It's not just a myth. Bloody hell, no wonder the men in this town treat women like whores, if that's all it takes. They don't even have to stalk the meal; it just comes hopping into their den and jumps in the pan. All they have to do is drop the name of a famous connected friend and batta-bing batta-boom, they're in. Geez, what chance does a decent girl have?

In a town where most people live on the edge of greatness or despair, where in one encounter your life can be made or destroyed, people become very adept at using anything they have to tip the scales in their favor. For many females, this means using their bodies and sexuality. I call these girls the fuckables. These are the girls who want success, fame, or fortune at any cost. The fuckable knows that the most powerful tool she has is her body and men's desire for it, so she uses it. I suppose for the rare girl, the lying down method is working and landing them in the places they want to be, but for the majority, they're giving it up and gaining nothing. Most of them are simply putting miles on their car and getting no closer to their destination.

I'd always assumed the fuckables were the super sluts in high school. You know, the jaded girls who used sex to get what they wanted from the minute they discovered its power over the male of the species? But maybe that's not the case at all. Maybe some of these girls started out just like me.

Is it possible some of the fuckables were slightly naïve good girls with big dreams that were used against them? Is it possible that, like me, they came to Hollywood from their hometown convinced that their "it-ness" would be noticed just by walking down the street, or buying groceries? They just knew that if the right person saw them, the rest would be history. After months or years of working their asses off trying to get an agent, manager, audition, etc., and seeing no results, they came to a place of true desperation and sold out when they confronted a situation like the one I just encountered.

Sure, they knew on some level when they made the choice that they were whoring themselves out for the audition, reading, shot. They knew they would have to put out to get it, but they thought in their misguided minds that they were so unique, beautiful, and captivating that when the director saw them, he would fall under their oh-so-special spell and turn them into stars. In desperation, they decided the end justified the means, and they began the long slippery slide down the slope to becoming a fuckable.

What a horrid thought!

I need a drink.

Reaching the bottom of the hill, I swerve into the Mayfair Market parking lot. It may be the most expensive store in town, but it is also the closest, and desperate times call for even more desperate purchases. Time to bust out the emergency credit card and buy a bottle of vino.

Before I run in, I text the German: *Disaster! On my way over.*

"You okay?" she texts back.

Not really. Tell all when I arrive.

"Okay babe. I love you."

As I wait in line to pay for my consolation prize for the night, I notice the pack of cigarettes the gentleman in front of me is buying. I haven't seen a cigarette pack in a while, and the massive new warning label printed on it must be visible from space. I've gotta admit, if those warning labels didn't tell me how bad smoking was, I could easily see myself having a clove cigarette addiction. They taste so good and give you such a great buzz. It's just kind of hard to justify picking up a habit you have been informed in advance will kill you slowly and painfully.

Suddenly it hits me. That's what we need! If these sneaky dream predators had a warning label tattooed on them, maybe a lot of good girls could be saved from becoming fuckables. Sure, I managed to escape the trap laid for me, but it's easy to see why a lot of girls don't. Maybe they're really beat down from trying so hard and facing so much rejection. Maybe they don't have the inner fortitude gifted to them by a strong family. Maybe they just are too scared to say no. Maybe if they had been warned in advance, they would have run from the soul thief before the trap was even laid.

Time to give them a warning. There's only one problem. I don't see the manipulative liars lining up to have "Dream Predator" tattooed on their foreheads.

The cashier rings up a half-gallon of milk. The face of a missing child stares at me from the carton.

Voilà! That's it. The German and I will ask the milk companies to let us use the other side of the carton, and we'll print the faces of dream predators in Hollywood with a warning label.

I can see the campaign now.

"Find a lost child. Prevent a lost soul. Do a body good."

Solo Performance [**sō**-lō pə(r)-**fȯr**-mən(t)s]
noun

1. The erotic stimulation of one's own peach-ca or cock, commonly resulting in orgasm. Climax is achieved by manual or other bodily contact exclusive of sexual intercourse, by instrumental manipulation, occasionally by sexual fantasies, or by various combinations of these agencies.

2. That's right, just a better name for good old-fashioned masturbation.

Example: "The long-distance lovers were forced to engage in solo performances far too often."

IT PEEKS FOR ITSELF

"Okay, we are going to call it 'Dan.'"

Oh geez. This is not happening. They're not naming my butt, and if they are, surely they could pick a better name than "Dan." At least a girl's name, for goodness' sake.

"So, if anyone has a Charity ass-sighting, holler 'Dan' so we can all get in on the action."

Big Picture drills the guys on the protocol while I tug the world's shortest dress down, wondering if maybe I didn't go a little too far this time.

I've an obsession with baby-doll dresses. The higher the altitude of the hemline, the more I love them. I frequently stand in dressing rooms orchestrating my favorite dance moves while peering over my shoulder into the mirror to decide which category they go into: the Dance Doll or the Dinner Doll.

Dance Dolls are just long enough to raise my arms and still cover the bottom of my butt cheeks. Dinner Dolls are so short I can't even give someone a hug without flashing my ass-ettes. I prefer Dance Dolls because there is always a huge risk of me busting out my groove thing anytime, anyplace, anywhere. I'm completely incapable of holding still when a good song plays. Like the Pavlovian dog, the bell rings, the beat starts, and my body begins twitching. Next thing you know, I'm whirling, twirling, and pulsating. On nights where there is a bit too much alcohol involved, I can even be found busting into my own version of *Footloose* on the table, or any elevated surface that could possibly be misinterpreted as a stage. That being said, it's not wise for me to buy Dinner Dolls!

Despite this, every once in a while I come across one that is so beautiful, so perfect, I have to have it. In those cases, I throw caution to the wind and purchase it anyway, hoping for the best. That was the case with this dress. The real question is, what made me think I could get away with wearing it today of all days?

It's Cowgirl's wedding, and hundreds of people have flown in from all over the world to celebrate at the Bohemian Grove in the middle of the Redwood Forest. To give you a visual, it feels like George Lucas's Ewok village in *Return of the Jedi*. There is a mammoth owl-shaped altar carved out of the remains of a tree, a pond surrounded by torches and overgrown trails, and villages of hundreds of wooden huts nestled among the towering redwoods. I've been anticipating this wedding all year. That is, until two weeks ago, when the Man, my boyfriend of the last eight months, broke up with me.

From the instant I met the Man, I've been heels over head in love with him. That is to say that my heels were often over my head while loving him, and that's definitely not a bad thing!

We met at a New Year's Eve party in the Hollywood Hills. It was a dinner party of approximately twenty-four guests, almost all of them couples. I was a last-minute addition. My new friend, Miss Elegance, had called me earlier that day to wish me a Happy New Year. Upon discovering that my plans for the evening involved a box of Kleenex and a pity party, she'd insisted I join her and her husband at the dinner party they were attending. I resisted. Who wants to go to a party where you will be surrounded by happy couples when you are still recovering from a heart smash? In fact, the reason I was party-less was because I'd just been informed earlier that morning that some genius had invited Brown Eyes to the party I was planning on attending with Stunt Girl. The German was out of town. I feared if I saw Brown Eyes at a party, there was real danger of me ripping his eyes out for those stripper rumors he created. Call me crazy, but prison time for assault didn't seem like the wisest way to start the New Year. Hence the impromptu pity-party plans.

Miss Elegance insisted, "Though I'm sure a pity party is an absolutely viable alternative, I would encourage you to step out and try a 'real' party tonight."

In my weakened state I caved. I would go.

From the minute I walked into the bustling room of party guests, I could feel the Man's gaze. A tall, solitary figure dressed in all black, he stood out from the crowd. He studied me from across the room throughout the entire cocktail hour. I was as aware of him as he was of me, but I feigned ignorance, waiting for him to come to me. To let him know I was receptive, I gave the occasional flirtatious laugh with eye contact. Despite that, he never moved. Every fiber of my being was tuned into that sexy man. It was surreal. I desperately wanted to meet him, but I couldn't initiate. I firmly believe that the man has to do the hunting, not the woman. In my experience, men never value the things that come to them too easily. If they really want you, they will come after you. So I waited. He never approached. I was on pins and needles.

At dinner, the hostess directed us all to assigned seats. Hallelujah! Thank my fairy godmother—mine was right next to the Man's! I guess that was no big surprise, as we were the only single people in the entire room, but I was elated. I was also trembling with nerves. After we were introduced, the Man graciously pulled out my chair and gestured for me to sit. As I carefully folded my long legs into the chair, attempting not to give away my excitement, he leaned over and whispered into my ear, "Let's have a love affair. At least to start with."

So much blood rushed to my head that I almost fainted. Dropping to my seat, I put my hands up to cover my burning face. That was the hottest thing anyone had ever said to me and he, a complete stranger, had done it right in front of the whole table without anyone knowing. That was bold. I love bold men.

I was in!

What a love affair it was! The most magical, amazing, intense, inspiring, sexy relationship I'd ever had. We loved in Los Angles, Paris, Zurich, and Montreux. In beds, vineyards, dungeons, and sex clubs. We laughed, talked, dreamed, and played our way through swaths of the world. He turned out to be every bit as amazing as I'd dreamed he was on that starry New Year's Eve from across the room. I adored him.

There was only one problem; one little fly in the ointment, one little thorn on the rose. It pertained to issues of proximity. My tall, dark, handsome stranger had the temerity to live on a different continent. To be precise, he lived in Switzerland. What was it with me and Swiss men?

Due to the distance, our romance was made up of vast amounts of yearning and transitory moments of fulfillment. Our times apart were filled with epic love letters, phone calls, and iChat. Our times together were filled with lovemaking, laughter, and urgency. We had the kind of love affair they write books about, or to be more specific, the kind of love affair that only lasts in books.

Yes, okay, on some level I knew he was right; it could not go on forever that way. Either I would have to move to Switzerland, he would have to move to LA, or the unthinkable: we would have to call it quits. There were too many nights alone, too many missed moments, too much investment for too little return. It was probably easier for me to go on in that state indefinitely because, after all, I was in Tinsel Town. Sure, I was lonely for missing him, but not truly alone. This city whirs in a never-ending rotation of parties, events, and dinners. My nights were spent with friends, and my days were spent writing, so I didn't feel the holes in the relationship as much as he did. He was in Zurich, where, let's face it, there is not as much excitement or fun. Not to mention the never-ending rainy, gray skies make an actual physical lover—and not one at the end of an iChat line—far more essential. It's not that I didn't see all these things. It's just that I didn't want to see them.

Why would I want to? Never in my life had I encountered a man like him. He was an *original* original. The real deal. On top of that, there was ample evidence to suggest that he might actually be smitten with the real me, and not just my packaging. In my experience, men primarily loved me for my beauty, not my being. Then they proceeded to project all their desires onto me. Few actually saw me instead of their own fantasies, and when they did, they'd get mad at me for being exactly who I'd always been.

The Man was different.

I have this crystal-clear memory of a cold, rainy February night in Paris, lying in bed with the Man. I was bummed because my friend, Swiss Miss, had rejected a series of articles about dating in Los Angeles I'd written for a Swiss newspaper. She told me she wouldn't submit them; they were unprofessional, and the writing style needed years of work before it would be any good. I was crushed. I'd desperately hoped that I'd finally found an outlet for my writing and a way to make a living instead of scraping by, and here, my dear friend, a professional journalist, was telling me my stuff was a steaming pile of shit. I told the Man what had happened, and he asked to read one of the articles.

"Hell, no, do I look like a glutton for punishment?" I groaned.

I sure as hell didn't need any more criticism. The Man, like Swiss Miss, had the aggravating tendency of being brutally honest. Normally I found that an endearing character trait, but my Swiss Miss encounter had me seriously reconsidering the value of candy-coating. I was past the end of my rope and clutching to that tiny little piece of fuzz that dangles from the bottom. A stiff breeze could have knocked me into the abyss. I wasn't about to give the Man any reason to blow.

I was no match for the formidable will of the Man, though. Before I knew it, he had a copy of one of the stories in his hand and was reading away. Bursts of laughter and head shakes accompanied his eyes perusing the page. Actually laughing at me to my face? Seriously? Now that was going too far. Even the Swiss Miss didn't do that. I buried my head under the covers and waited for the inevitable literary assault that would come at the end of the story. When he finished, he slammed the pages down onto the tangled sheets and jumped to his feet. Then he let it rip.

"It's genius! Brilliant! I love it!"

Surely he must be teasing. If it was so great, why would Swiss Miss have found it so awful? I peeked out from the covers to see when the punch line was coming, but he was just getting started. Pacing back and forth like a caged tiger, he continued.

"Charity Gaye Finnestad, you have an original voice! Do you know how rare that is?"

Butterflies flooded my tummy. This didn't feel like the buildup to a punch line. This felt like the beginning of one of the Man's tirades, and the Man was nothing if not deadly serious about his tirades.

"I read all the time. I see everything that's out there. Most of it is uninspired and unoriginal. All the life has been trained out of it. There's no voice. You, my dear, have a voice. I would read this. It's great. It makes me laugh. It makes me feel. It's sexy as hell. I want more…"

"Are you serious?"

"I've never been more! Who knew I was fucking such a talent?"

I started laughing. I catapulted myself onto him—legs and arms wrapped around. We tumbled to the bed. The smile that filled my insides leaked out my toes. I wanted to jump up and down on the mattress and do a million Yippy Skippys. Sure, I was still where I started, with nowhere to sell my writing and no way of making a living from it, but I had my first reader!

The Man wasn't finished. His tirade was just getting started. Boy, what a tirade it was! The best he'd ever delivered. That tiny Paris apartment couldn't contain it, or the joy oozing out of us. Before I knew it, we were bundled up in clothes, heading out into the dark, rainy streets of Paris to plot, plan, and dream about where my original voice would take me. Not to mention how I was going to get it out there. Halfway through the night, the Man became convinced that I needed to do a blog. He loved the name I'd come up with, *Hollywood in Heels*, and was certain that if I started blogging my stories, they would get a following. I was skeptical. He was adamant.

"Charity. You have to do this. There are no guarantees in life, but you have a real chance at making it. Trust me. You need to do it."

Two bottles of wine later, I was convinced.

The Man proceeded to elicit a promise from me to do two stories a week for six months, regardless of what happened. If I would do it, he would sponsor it. It was outrageous. It would be a lot of work. I probably wouldn't have the time or energy to write anything else. It was risky and crazy. My whole life would be exposed. If my writing really was shit, I would find out right away. Better to know now if I needed to give up my dream and change course, rather than years down the road. Besides, maybe, just maybe, there were more people like the Man than Swiss Miss. Maybe, just maybe, there were people out there who would like my writing. What a glorious thought. I would do it!

Six months later, my blog was going full steam ahead. It had indeed changed my life. Within two months of posting my first story, I was contacted by one of the most powerful agencies in LA. They wanted to talk about turning my blog into a TV series. Little old me who couldn't even get her big toe in the door of the crappiest agencies in town was being pursued by the big shots. It was crazy! From writing all alone in the Fairy Cottage to actually having readers and a possible series of my own. All because the Man believed in me. He saw more than his own reflection. He valued the artist, not just the muse, and he fought to help her have her day in the sun. Sure, I was the one who had to do the work (as he kept pointing out), but without him, I wouldn't even have known where to start.

The Man was my hero. I loved him to the moon.

That's why, two weeks ago, when he decided to end our relationship, I felt like the sun had been turned off. My international man of mystery, my champion, my lover, my friend—gone. He informed me he could no longer bear the bi-continental nature of the relationship. He was too lonely too much of the time. I tried to fool myself and him that I would give it all up and move to Switzerland, but he wouldn't let me do it.

"You are young and on fire," he said. "The whole world is opening for you. I won't let you throw it away to come hole up with me in Switzerland. I believe in you too much. You need to be in LA."

I knew he was right, but I was devastated. I couldn't imagine my life without him. On top of that, we were supposed to attend this over-the-top wedding together. Now I was attending it alone, freshly broken-hearted. Not exactly an ideal scenario for a hopeful romantic like myself.

That's where the dress comes in. I have this theory that if you look good, you greatly increase your chances of feeling good. I had it long before moving to Hollywood, but Hollywood definitely reinforced it. I've discovered that oftentimes, when I feel the worst, I unconsciously make an effort to look the best. Like war paint and armor; makeup, cute clothes, and high heels protect me from being too vulnerable and exposed. They give me that extra psychological edge I need to go into battle, or the grocery store, or a wedding, or whatever the hurdle of the moment.

Marguerite Harrison, the first documentary filmmaker and an absolutely amazing woman, kept her sanity by using her vanity as a means of maintaining her identity when she was held as a war spy in Russia's infamous Lubyanka Prison for ten months. Confined to a tiny, cold, stone cell, day in and day out, she found one simple way to remind herself who she was. She ripped the bottom of her dress into strips and created rag curlers. Regardless of how tired and defeated she felt, every night, she put her hair up in those curlers. Then before her daily interrogations, she would take them out and arrange her hair. By this one defiant act, she was able to control her world, maintain a sense of self, and come out unbroken.

I suppose that, somehow, by wearing this attention-grabbing dress, I'm doing the same. People won't even think of giving me pity and condolences when they're busy teasing me about my minidress. I've changed the energy I will receive and by doing that, changed the way I'll feel.

Teasing is not bad. I grew up with brothers. I know it's a form of affection. It makes you laugh, and laughter is still the best medicine. Which makes me wonder—maybe in our attempts to help others, we actually do more harm than good. Maybe instead of doling out pity and commiserating with our friends who, for example, fight cancer, we should give them shit about their bald noggins. I don't know; I could be very wrong, but it is at least something to consider. I think one of the most terrible things on the planet is pity. It encourages self-pity, and I don't know about you, but the one time I really don't like myself is when I'm practicing self-pity.

Suddenly the German, who arrived earlier than me and knows my trepidation about being here, runs up and grabs me in an embrace. As I return her hug, I hear shouts from two different sides,

"Dan!"

"Dan!"

Quickly dropping my arms and tugging my dress down, I dissolve into giggles.

"What's that about?" the German queries.

"They've named my ass."

"Dan? Really? Couldn't they do better than that? A girl's name at least?" Turning toward the men, the German shouts, "Hey boys, I'd like to introduce you to Patty." Then she promptly yanks up her skirt and flashes her ass-ettes.

When I can finally stop laughing enough to breathe, I realize this is going to be one hell of a party. I'm going to have a full-time job keeping the German from flashing Patty and my butt from peeking for itself. One thing is certain though; I won't be crying about the Man's absence tonight. The tears will have to wait for another time. I haven't failed to notice that there are a lot of older gentlemen here, and I do not want to be responsible for any heart attacks. It's one thing to cause a commotion. It's another to cause a coronary. Okay, let the celebration begin! Where's the bloody champagne?

Are you in love with love?

Do you find yourself suffering from a severe addiction to affection? Can you be found in corners kissing frogs, thinking they will turn into princes? Is your addiction interfering with your life, friendships, work, and the pursuit of your dream? If you answered yes to one or more of these questions, we can help.

Join the Hollywood branch of F.L.A.P. (Functioning Love-Aholics Public) and say goodbye to your addiction to love once and for all. We offer a non-judgmental, cure-directed support group designed to enable you to overcome the crippling affects of your mental illness. We meet every Friday night at nine p.m. at Hemingway's in Hollywood. Attendance is open, there are no dues, and we find privacy unnecessary. Why kid ourselves? There is nothing anonymous about us.

F.L.A.P.

Well, it's official; my sickness has been diagnosed and labeled. Okay, sure, it was self-diagnosis, but it has to count for something. At least now I've developed a term for my disease so that I have a permanent excuse for all of my future bad behavior.

Don't you love how that works? A person can flake on you and say, "I'm ADD," and suddenly you are no longer allowed to be outraged by their disrespect for your time and the fact that they blew off an engagement without even a phone call. Depression means they can sulk and mope constantly, totally refusing to laugh even when you show up at their door sporting a big red clown nose, willing to make a fool of yourself for a smile. Bipolar means they can Dr. Jekyll you one moment and Mr. Hyde you the next. And last but not least, alcoholic means you get to go to the best meetings in Hollywood and hang out with movie stars up close and personal. Yep, no doubt about it; my neurosis needed a name so I can get away with murder and form my own club. So are you ready? Here it is. Drum roll please...

"I'm a functioning love-aholic."

Don't laugh. I'm serious! I was pretty clear on the love-aholic part, but the functioning part just came to me right now.

I'm sitting at dinner with the Professor and his beautiful new girlfriend, Ray of Light, a gifted psychologist. I just got done talking their ears off for two solid hours about my love life adventures (man, they're good sports), and at the end I asked, "Do you think I'm addicted to love?"

After laughing, Ray of Light queried, "Well, are you functioning? We make a distinction between addicts who are functioning and those who are not."

"Sure, at the moment, but I've definitely been in the non-functioning phase. I've been curled up in a ball, crying my eyes out, not leaving my house, and unable to eat after a couple of my major heartbreaks. I think that would qualify as non-functioning."

With a smile, trying to break it to me softly she says, "Well, sweetie, I think it has to be a chemical thing to qualify as an addiction."

Hell no! I'm not backing down that quickly. "Geez, are you trying to tell me those happy juices flooding my brain with idiotic ideas when I'm in love are not chemical? Because I'd bet you anything they are."

The Professor nods. Yippy Skippy, I think I won a convert. Ray of Light still looks unconvinced about my determination to have a psychological label for my disorder. Apparently she is unaware of how handy labels can be. They're essential for explaining away things.

I ought to make that point for all of the people who roll their eyes when I ask them for their star sign. By laughing off astrology, they're throwing away a perfectly good excuse for all of their bad behavior. I mean, let's face it; every one of the star signs has a list of flaws a mile long that can easily be used to justify one's actions. Imagine with me a courtroom where a woman born, oh, let's say November 6th, is being tried for bashing in the brains of her husband's lover with a garden gnome. The prosecution lays out an airtight case against her. She sits on the witness stand, tearfully confessing to the truth of the accusations. Then, in a stroke of pure genius, her defense attorney says, "Ladies and gentlemen of the jury. You have heard all the evidence against my client. You have even heard her confess to the murder, but what you haven't heard is the most important piece of evidence in this case! You see, the defendant was born on November 6th, which makes her... a Scorpio."

A gasp is heard from the direction of the jury, and an eerie silence falls over the room. The defense attorney continues, "Anyone who knows anything about astrology knows that Scorpios are incredibly possessive and jealous by nature. It was therefore a totally natural reaction for her to lose her mind and kill the woman cheating with her husband. Frankly, I think we should applaud her for restraining herself and not killing him as well. How can you possibly hold this crime against her when the very timing of her birth gives her no other alternative but to act this way when confronted with infidelity? Her actions, although unfortunate, were not her fault. To punish her for this crime would be to punish her for the day she was born. How can you, in clear conscience, find her guilty for her own birth? You have no other choice but to find the defendant... not guilty by reason of astrology."

The courtroom bursts into applause, and the defendant gets off scot-free. Legal precedent changes forever. Astrology is taken into consideration in every trial. Come on, if temporary insanity is a reason to not be punished for a crime, then permanent astrology should definitely be a legitimate excuse. I know I'd use it!

But I digress. The important thing here is not astrology, it's my diagnosis. If I'm a functioning love-aholic, then I can no longer be harassed for my hopeful romantic streak and my panache for getting into intense relationships without much thought for the possible outcome. I also cannot be condemned for my total inability to let go of people. It's obvious that a love-aholic will never stop loving someone; just like an alcoholic is always an alcoholic.

Look at me right now. I'm sitting at dinner with the Professor, who I still love deeply (although now it's in a non-sexual, familial way). I'm still madly in love with the Man (though we are categorically just friends). And I'm contemplating falling in love with a new (yet to be determined) guy. What is wrong with me? Clearly Ray of Light is wrong, and I'm in fact a certifiable, full-fledged case of a functioning love-aholic.

Well, anyway, that's my story, and I'm sticking to it. Who needs a professional diagnosis when I can self-analyze and come up with my own? So, if you should ever find me in compromising positions, kissing frogs in corners hoping they will turn into princes, that's my excuse. Take me or leave me, but don't expect to change me. I may be functioning, but I'm obviously a lifetime love-aholic.

Seven Signs a Relationship has Reached its
Sex-piration Date:

1. Sex is no longer good.
2. Sex is no longer happening.
3. Sex is the only thing that is good about the relationship.
4. You no longer like your partner.
5. Your partner no longer likes you.
6. You fight more than you fuck.
7. You're not happy.

BUILT-IN SEX-PIRATION

I look across the table at one of the most amazing men I've met in a long time, Mr. Imagine. We've been seeing each other for a month, and unfortunately I have a bomb to drop on him. The dilemma is, I'm so nervous that I can't get the words out. I keep waiting for the right opening, and of course, I choose the very worst one. He says something about sex, and like an idiot, I blurt out, "Speaking of sex, I need to tell you something."

The minute the words leave my lips, I get all choked up and tears start leaking from my eyes. A look of absolute terror flashes across his face. I don't know if it's my statement, which is an absolute minefield of possibilities, or the tears (which are a guaranteed way to scare the bejesus out of any grown man), but he does not look comfortable. I don't blame him. In his situation, I wouldn't be either. Oh geez, I'm screwing this whole thing up. I meant to handle it in a savvy, sophisticated, big-city-girl way, and here I am being the regular sensitive, overly emotional Charity.

"Um, what I meant (choked-up voice) to say is, speaking of sex... (uh-oh, are those tears I feel running down my face?)... tonight will be the last night of it. (Now I'm a regular faucet, complete with sniffles, hiccups, and mascara smears, and his discomfort grows in direct proportion to my water output.) What I mean is, tonight is our last night as lovers, and I'm hoping tomorrow is our first day as dear friends."

Relief! I got it out! No matter what happens now, at least I had the courage to say exactly what I needed to. All I can hope is that he is as classy and amazing as I think he is and can deal with this surprising turn of events. I feel terrible. I'm positive he didn't see it coming. How could he? I didn't either, until a few days ago.

I was on a hike, thinking about my life and all of the relationships I'd been in, when a realization came to me. Every man I'd ever dated had a built-in sex-piration date. A guaranteed life span—that was not my whole life. It sounds crazy, but it's true. On some organic level I knew all of them were going to end. Which meant none of them were quite the right fit.

What really blew my mind was the realization that generally speaking, I picked hard-to-get, emotionally unavailable guys who I knew would leave me, so I wouldn't be forced to do what I'm doing right now and say good-bye to them. I'd much rather be the dumpee than the dumper. I hate hurting or disappointing someone, especially someone I love, and I never get involved with a man unless I love him. Knowing that the men I fell in love with would leave gave me complete freedom to dive all the way in without fear of being trapped with the wrong one.

I remember a conversation I'd had with Jamie Kennedy five years ago when he said, "Men keep their options open and date a ton of women at the same time until they find the one who has everything they want, then they drop the rest. Women generally pick one man, take him for a full relationship test drive, and then dump him when he doesn't pass all their inspection points."

I don't know about other women, but he was dead-on accurate about me. I fall for one guy at a time, and I go through the whole process with him before realizing it's not quite right for me. The problem is, I never have the courage to pull the emergency ejection switch at the moment of discovery. Instead, I stay in the plane and go down in a crash of romantic flames and glory.

It's my own fault. I just get too attached. I've been known to stay in a relationship years past its sex-piration date. The problem with this mode of operation is that life is short, and I really do want a shot at the real thing someday. If I keep investing big chunks of my life and time in the not-quite-right fits, I may never find the perfect match.

When that lightbulb went off, I knew I had to call an end to things with my current flame, Mr. Imagine. Unlike the emotionally unavailable men I normally go for, he was the real deal, a man who could handle a meaningful relationship. The problem was, though he was a close fit, one of the sexiest men I'd met in years, and a guy who felt like family instantly, he was not the perfect match. Every girl knows that a shoe that is a close fit may feel just fine at first, but over time will start to cause discomfort and eventually extreme pain. I don't want that with Mr. Imagine. I treasure him and want to keep him in my life. The real question is, does he feel the same way about me?

"I knew something was coming, but I wasn't expecting that." Mr. Imagine finally says.

He candidly shares his thoughts and feelings about us, and I share mine. By the end of dinner, I know why I like him so much. When I ask him if he still wants to be my friend, if that's all I can offer, he says, "Absolutely."

Relief floods my whole system, and I tear up again. Thank god! I didn't want to lose him. I love the man.

Classy, sexy, and confident, he leans across the table, raises his eyebrows, and parries, "So you said tonight is our last night, right?"

"Yes."

"Then don't count on sleeping."

D.M.F. (Dominant Mother Fucker)

A breed of man who, without a second thought, will rip up your skirt and take you in the bathroom at your parents' house during Thanksgiving dinner, all the while getting off on the inappropriateness of it.

Example: "That D.M.F. ordered me to take off my clothes, put on a pair of heels, and go wait for him upstairs."

*K*nock, knock.

I'm yanked from a deep sleep by a pounding on my front door. I look at my phone. It's nine a.m. Who could be coming over at this hour? I crawl out of bed and tug a sweatshirt on over the Rock & Republic tank top and boy shorts I received in a goodie bag last week. Just what I need; a surprise visitor to see me in my sick, disheveled state. I've been running a fever, coughing, and blowing my nose all night. I'm in no shape for company.

I crack open the front door and see the back of a delivery boy lumbering down the stairs. Must have been a wrong address. As I go to close the door, I notice a flash of yellow out of the corner of my eye. Looking down, I see a giant, three-foot basket wrapped in yards of cellophane. What on Earth? I rip open the wrapping and discover chicken soup, crossword puzzles, candy aspirin, NyQuil, DayQuil, Advil, a box of Kleenex, and all kinds of other feel-better ingredients. It's the most thoughtful gift I've ever received.

On pins and needles, I dig through the basket looking for the card. Spotting the envelope, I tear it open. There, in Times New Roman type, are words that could very well change my whole life...

"I get it. It's about trust. Just let me know the instant you trust me.

The Music Man"

Throwing the envelope in the air, I kiss the card and burst into the biggest Yippy Skippy in the history of Yippy Skippys, complete with a war cry, a wracking cough, and joy-filled laughter that echoes across the canyon. This goes on long enough for the neighbors to call the funny farm to haul me off if they're so inclined. Thank goodness they aren't. I tumble onto the wicker rocking chair on my porch, almost crying with happiness. This card is proof that the Music Man may very well be my real-life Magic Man. Holy shit! I can barely believe it.

Two nights ago when I met him, I had him pinned as a real D.M.F. I certainly didn't imagine he was the chicken soup, crossword-puzzle type.

It was Halloween weekend, and the Man in Black, being a good friend as always, had invited me out for a fun-filled adventure. We were to attend the Murakami opening at MOCA's Geffen Contemporary. Dinner at Koi, followed by drinks and dancing at a costume party. I'd asked the Man in Black if the Producer, the fellow I'd been seeing for the last couple of weeks, could tag along. He said, "Sure." When I extended the invitation to the Producer he said, "I have a meeting. I can't attend the opening, but I'll try to pop by Koi later."

After thoroughly enjoying the Murakami exhibit, the Man in Black, dressed as Napoleon, and I, dressed as a French whore, headed to Koi to meet up with the rest of our crew who'd skipped the art opening. When we arrived, a half a dozen of the Man in Black's model entourage and a guy I'd never seen before were waiting for us at our table. Everyone in the entire establishment was regaled in some kind of Halloween costume: sexy Bo-peep, Darth Vader, gangsters, sexy vampires, scary monsters, sexy nun, etc. Everyone except the guy I'd never seen before. He wore a black tee-shirt and blue jeans. He was quite conspicuous for his normalcy. The Man in Black, far more exuberant than normal, grabbed the costume-less fellow in a bear hug when we reached the table. Then he proceeded to introduce him to the rest of us. "Meet the Music Man. One of the most powerful guys in the industry, and one of my best friends."

That was a surprise; not the power part, because everyone the Man in Black knows is powerful, but the best friend part. I'd met loads of women through the Man in Black, but very few men he called a close friend. This guy must have been pretty special if the Man in Black loved him.

The Music Man shook my hand and gave me a very male once-over. That wasn't shocking—after all, I was terribly risqué in my garters, stockings, corset, and feathered red costume. Like all the other girls in the dark enclave of Koi, my costume screamed, "Slut." What was surprising was my response. As his intense gaze raked my body, I literally felt an electric jolt go down my spine. That never happened. Surprised and curious, I sat next to him.

I knew it was dangerous. I couldn't resist.

Normally when I was that drawn to a man, it was because he was a bad boy, also known as a D.M.F. I think it goes back to caveman times where the dominant males who were most likely to get you pregnant ruled female hearts and bodies. It's evidenced even in modern elementary school; the boys who pull your pigtails are the ones you crush on. Even better is the secret knowledge handed down to girls by mothers and teachers that the boy pulling your pigtail is doing so because he likes you. That's enough to make every schoolgirl's heart pitter-patter. It doesn't end there though; most girls spend the rest of their lives being powerfully drawn to dominant men who will pull their hair.

I was no exception.

The catch was, I was drawn to that type, but I didn't want to live with them. My DNA might have craved the one who could produce the strongest offspring, but my brain told me to go with the civilized, nurturing one who could help me lovingly raise that offspring. I wanted the guy who would pull my hair in bed and then hold it out of the toilet when I was sick. In short, I wanted a Pirate/Prince, not one or the other. The big dilemma was that very few men know how to embody both. Most men have had the pirate trained right out of them, and the ones who haven't don't normally have a single princely bone in their entire body. It was really a tragedy. Despite the slim odds, I refused to give up hope that someday I would find one. If I didn't, I was never settling down again.

The Music Man and I were eyebrow-deep in conversation the instant my butt hit the seat next to him. The rest of the world vanished as we parried words and flirted outrageously. The Man in Black could barely get a word in edgewise, and the table of gorgeous models ceased to exist. I was drowning in the deep waters of chemical attraction. I hadn't been so high on magic in a long time.

An hour and a half into our interlude, I was ripped out of my euphoria by a tap on my shoulder. It was the Producer. Before I could say a word, he grabbed me for a long deep kiss. I'd forgotten all about him! With dread, I turned and saw the look on the Music Man's face. The Producer draped his arm proprietarily around my back and slid into the booth on the other side of me. I was paralyzed. Introductions were made. The Music Man, after greeting the Producer, turned his back to me and started chatting with the Man in Black and the table full of models. He made it very clear our conversation was over; as if it had never happened.

I was freaking out!

Sure, I really liked the Producer, that's why we were having a fling, but I'd come to the conclusion very quickly that he was not my guy. He was not the Magic Man. Who knew if the Music Man was; he might just be another pirate without a princely bone in his body, but I had this really sick feeling in my stomach that not finding out would be a disaster. I desperately wanted to tell the Music Man, "We're not serious. He's just a lover. Don't ignore me!" But my respect for the Producer and my belief system that the man has to do the pursuing wouldn't allow it.

So I remained silent, going through the motions of enjoying the evening.

I was suffering! It was one of the worst nights ever. Every minute felt like an eternity. I'd made my stupid sex-filled bed, and I was lying in it.

My heart screamed that there was a very real chance that my choosing to be with the flavor of the moment was going to prevent me from finding my Pirate/Prince of a lifetime. It was too late though. There was nothing I could do. I had to let go. If the Music Man was my guy, it would figure itself out.

Three endless hours later, as the night approached the dawn and the party started to wind down, it happened. We were at Winstons, our third venue for the evening. I was making my way back from the bathroom, about to tell everyone that it was my pumpkin hour, when the Music Man stopped me in the hallway. The thumping base of Justin Timberlake's "Sexy Back" dimmed to a purr, and the thronging masses of costumed bodies jostling around us receded into the background as he spoke.

"The Man in Black explained your situation to me. I never want to disrespect another man, but I really like you. I think we need to see each other again."

Then he extended his hand, placed a business card in mine, closed my fingers over it, and walked away.

Every bone in my body melted.

He was so bloody confident. I was excited and scared at the same time. That night when I got home I sent everyone, including the Music Man, pictures I'd taken throughout the evening. Now he had my contact info.

The next morning (yesterday), I woke up with a burning sore throat, a fever, and a horrid cough. Talk about bad timing. When I opened my email, a message from the Music Man flashed up:

Let me take you to dinner tonight.

Bummed, I wrote back: *I'd love to, but I'm sick.*

His response: *It's my last night in town. I'll take you out for chicken noodle soup at six and have you home by eight.*

I knew he lived in San Francisco, and if I said no, I might never see him again. That couldn't happen. I said yes.

Sure enough, at five minutes to six last night, the Music Man knocked on my front door for what would officially be our first date. He brought me to a little café called Home near the Fairy Cottage and ordered me a steaming bowl of chicken noodle soup. Having grown completely fed up with the massive quantities of bullshit I'd consumed over the years of dating in Hollywood, I decided to do a completely novel thing. Bypassing the toe-in-the-water temperature-testing normal people use in relationships, I hurled myself cannonball style off the deep end of truth. Imagine my surprise and delight when I came up for air and saw his glowing body flying through the air to join me. Sparking like crazy, we proceeded at a hundred and twenty miles an hour down a road I'd never attempted to travel with any other man—the unvarnished truth. There was no small talk. No evasions. No illusions. No initial dance. No pretending. We skipped the shallow end completely, and went straight into reality. Our dreams, our strengths, our weaknesses, our failings, our successes, and our desires were revealed with nothing held back. I even told him I'd been married twice. I never told anyone that!

It was an amazing duel of honesty. The intensity was mind-blowing. One after the other, we parried each other with the truth. Neither one of us missed a beat. We presented ourselves with total transparency. Things most couples take years to reveal, we exposed in one night. If either one of us would have blinked and pulled the mask back on, even for just a second, I suspect the whole thing would have come undone. Neither of us did. The courage and passion we evidenced for each other was insane.

It was a dance like no other.

As promised, the Music Man had me home at eight. The date, however, did not end until two o'clock this morning. Despite the sparks flying between us, we never touched. We sat on my wicker rocking chair overlooking LA and talked. And talked. And talked. When my voice was a mere croak and I could no longer say a word, the Music Man kissed my forehead and insisted it was time he say goodnight. He was flying back to San Francisco at seven-thirty the next morning, but he promised to call after work.

I was so excited I couldn't sleep. I knew my whole life had just changed.

At five in the morning, I still couldn't sleep. Tossing and turning, suffering from severe exhaustion, my excitement turned to fear. What if he was a chameleon like Brown Eyes? What if he was not who he seemed to be? What if this was his "good foot?" What if? What if? Between the fever, the throat infection, and the questions, I was a hot mess. Crawling out of bed, determined to turn off the questions so I could finally sleep, I wrote him a letter guaranteed to scare the bejesus out of any grown man.

I took three long pages to tell him a horrifically honest thing,

"I normally sleep with a guy, then get to know him. In your case, it is going to be different. We are not sleeping together until I really know you. I don't think I could handle the damage if I gave you my body (on top of all this honesty) and you are not who you seem to be. We have to wait."

Unburdened, I hit "send" and fell into a deep sleep.

As I look at my wonderful care package now, a wave of total exhilaration rushes over my fevered body. I read the note again.

I get it. It's about trust. Just let me know the instant you trust me.

The Music Man

Bursting off the rocking chair, I jump into another Yippy Skippy. He didn't panic. I didn't scare him. He can handle it. He can handle me. He understands. He's willing to wait. I'm the luckiest girl alive. I may have just found one of the few living Pirate/Princes on the planet. If so, this could very well be the beginning of my Happily Ever After. I'll get to be his Slut/Princess. Now all I need to do is find out if I can really trust him. Time will reveal that. Then I'll get to see if my first instinct was right and he is, in fact, a D.M.F. Will he yank up my skirt and screw me in the history section of the public library, all the while covering my mouth and ordering me to be quiet (shiver, sigh)? If that's the case, I have just hit the Charity Jackpot!

I text the German, *You won't believe what just happened!* as I run into the bathroom to take a shower. I don't feel like lying in bed anymore. This line of thought is even better for curing sickness than DayQuil!

No doubt about it, I'm All Souped Up!

Hopeless = Having no expectation of good or success.

Romantic = A person whose creative work shows sensitivity and imagination.

Hopeless Romantic = A person with no expectation of good or success whose creative work shows sensitivity and imagination.

That sucks! I choose . . .

Hopeful = Having or expressing hope.

Romantic = A person whose creative work shows sensitivity and imagination.

Hopeful Romantic = A person of hope whose creative work shows sensitivity and imagination.

ROOTS AND WINGS

Holy shit! Is this really happening? I stare in awe at the twinkling Rockefeller Christmas Tree lights reflecting in the stunning engagement ring being offered to me. Oh, my goodness! This fairytale love story I have been living for the past month and a half just got incredibly real, incredibly fast.

Music Man and I are nearing the end of a three-week-long, jet-set, freeze-my-ass-off tour that has been one romantic haze of love and glory. It began with a jump across the pond to attend the mind-blowing Led Zeppelin reunion show in London. From there we hopped on a friend's private plane and flew to a ski adventure in Aspen. Next we braved a blizzard so he could meet my parents in Oregon. Now we're in the Big Apple under the influence of Kris Kringle, and I'm being offered the possibility of a Happily Ever After.

Staring at the Tiffany solitaire, as "Silent Night" plays in the background and shoppers jostle around us, a multitude of thoughts flash through my mind.

I love the Music Man. There's no question about that. We only met six weeks ago, but I feel like I've known him a million lifetimes. In that short time, I've learned a lot about who he is and what he's about.

First of all, he's hyper-intelligent. If that's not there, I don't even get wet. Second, he is passionate about everything he does. I've honestly never met anyone quite like him. The Music Man doesn't have dreams—he has plans, and he makes them happen. He's an inventor with numerous patents to his name, but you'd never know that. Ask the Music Man what he does for a living at a dinner party, and he'll give you an extremely downplayed answer. You'll walk away having no concept of the scale of his work and impact in the world. Like the Professor, he's a study in humility. Hollywood horn-blowing be damned. The Music Man doesn't like attention. He just wants to be left alone to build, build, build. He reminds me of Howard Roark in *The Fountainhead*. That alone is enough to make my nerd heart explode with desire, but that's not all.

Drum roll please…

The Music Man possesses integrity! He doesn't say anything he doesn't mean. He's the antithesis to the Tinsel Town prototype. He never sells a bill of goods he can't deliver. When he discusses a fairy castle in the sky, he's already figured out heavenly zoning codes, applied for the proper permits, and retained the best cloud construction crew available. He doesn't lie.

I got my first taste of the power of his word in Sin City two weeks after we met.

The Music Man was going to the opening of Koi Las Vegas, as was the Man in Black and his Flavor of the Moment girlfriend. The Music Man invited me to join; he wanted to spend time with me. I really wanted to go, but I'd meant what I said in the letter I sent him after our first date. I didn't want to get physical until I really knew him. Two weeks later, I still wasn't sure.

The Music Man promised to wait, but the whole Vegas invite combined with his pirate-y aura made me extremely skeptical of his intentions. Five years of dating Tinsel Town men had taken a toll on my trust.

"Do you think there is any chance he is not planning on seducing me?" I asked the German as we sat at Kings Road Café having lunch.

"No guy brings a girl to Vegas unless he intends to fuck her brains out." She took a bite of her burger. "Didn't you say you were pretty sure he was a pirate anyway?"

"Shit, I really thought I could trust him." I dropped my half-eaten bagel onto the plate.

The German saw I was distraught. "Look, maybe you can. Maybe he's a fucking saint. Honestly, Charity, you're totally in over your head with this guy anyway, and you've only known him two weeks. If he's a douche, you need to know! Go! Find out." Slugging down her Diet Coke, she continues. "Besides, I hear it's going to be one hell of a party."

She had a point. I was completely invested in this relationship. I had been from the moment I'd met him. Better to know now if I'd made a mistake than find myself in another Brown Eyes situation. I'd promised myself not to play that broken record ever again. I told the Music Man "yes." I would go.

Throughout the entire flight to Vegas, I drove the Man in Black and his Flavor of the Moment crazy with an onslaught of questions about the Music Man. "How do you know him?" "What do you think about him?" "Can I trust him?" "Has he asked about me?" "What did you say to him that night at Winstons?" I was a bloodhound for information. You can learn a lot about a man from his friends. Friends normally know the truth about you; not just the mask you show to the world. I was determined to ferret out whether the Music Man was wearing a mask with me, or if I was getting the real deal. Despite my reservations about Vegas, I'd not given up on the thought that Music Man might be my Magic Man. He'd certainly been saying all the right things.

By the time our plane landed in that dry patch of desert known as Sin City, I was giddy with anticipation. I would have to wait five long hours before I'd see the man I came to see, though. Unlike the rest of us, the Music Man had a grownup job with real business hours and couldn't come out to play until that evening. He would meet us at the opening party.

I knew the instant the Music Man walked into that crowded room of celebrities. I felt a prickle of awareness down my spine. Turning from my conversation with the Man in Black, I studied the crowd. Sure enough, there he was, standing in the entrance scanning the room. I waved. The Music Man returned my wave with a smile. I tried not to act excited as he headed our way, but I'm pretty sure I was glowing as bright as the light on top of the Luxor. Boy, I had it bad! Keep your panties on, Charity, I reminded myself.

The night was amazing! The four of us ate, drank, and danced our way to dawn. The German was right. It was one hell of a party. Somehow at the end of the evening I found myself alone with the Music Man in his suite at the Palms. How did that happen? Being there was a recipe for disaster. With the chemistry between us, I might as well have just thrown a lit match into a fuel truck. Brilliant, Charity, brilliant! One could hardly even blame him for what he was about to do. What man could resist a skimpily clad, high heel-sporting chick who was clearly madly in love with him when she was draped across his lap in a Vegas suite? Shit. I didn't know who was worse: him for building the spider web, or me for crawling right onto it. The worst part was, I knew I wouldn't say no. I wanted it as bad as he did, even though I knew I wasn't ready.

He didn't touch me.

That is to say, he didn't touch me sexually. Despite the lust-laden Vegas air filling our lungs, the Music Man didn't make a move. He held me in his arms and we talked. When I started to doze off, he called down for a car service to bring me to back to my room at the Planet Hollywood Hotel. He escorted me all the way to my door, then he gave me a peck on the cheek and said goodnight. I flung myself down on the hotel bed, exhausted but overwhelmed with happiness. I knew something big had just happened. The Music Man's honor was stronger than his lust. His word meant something. He just might be trustworthy.

Two weeks later, I got my final confirmation.

Music Man, his longtime friend Pretty Lady, and I were backstage at an Erykah Badu concert. I asked where the restroom was, and Pretty Lady offered to escort me. Once in the safety of the restroom, she turned and said, "Wow! I have never seen the Music Man like this about a woman. I've known him for ten years. I've seen him with every woman he's been involved with in that time, including his ex-wife, and I've never seen him like this. He's madly in love with you." Pretty Lady then proceeded to tell me how totally fantastic the Music Man was, finishing with a stern warning, "He's my dear friend and one of the most amazing men I know. You seem like a great girl, but I need to say this: You better be nice to him, or you will have me to deal with." I was so happy I could have done a Yippy Skippy right then and there.

Hands down, there was no better endorsement of a man's character available than one from an intelligent woman who had known him for years. I assured her I was madly in love with him, and in just as much danger of a heart smash as he. Then I grabbed her in a hug and thanked her for confirming that he was indeed the man he'd presented to me.

After the concert, standing on my porch bidding me farewell, the Music Man pressed his lips to my forehead and said, "I'm so glad I finally found you." Fireworks exploded! My knees dissolved! Since I was a girl, I'd secretly been writing letters to my Magic Man—even when I was married—even when I was in love. I always signed them, "Find Me." His words blasted my planet, spiraling it off its axis into the stratosphere. He turned and left. As he drove away from the Fairy Cottage I finally regained the ability to move. Digging through my purse, I located my phone and frantically texted him three little words: *I trust you.* Concise as ever, he texted back, *Meet me at the Beverly Hills Hotel, Wednesday night, at six.*

We were on.

That night, as I lay in bed drifting blissfully to sleep, a horrible thought yanked me awake. I bolted upright in bed. Shit! What if he had a small dick? Or was a bad lover? Oh, crap, why hadn't I thought of this?

I honestly had no clue, as we had been so circumspect about our physicality due to the sense that any spark would ignite an inferno. I should have at least pressed myself against him to cop a feel, or had the German do one of her amazingly accurate X-ray vision guesses. Not that I needed a giant, but I definitely enjoyed having something to work with. I was in so far over my head, what would I do if the sex wasn't good? I knew I couldn't live my whole life with bad sex!

Had I gone about this all wrong? Clearly my other way of going about it—sleeping with the guy, and then getting to know them—hadn't worked. Would this way be just as flawed? Realizing that I was once again going off the crazy board of paranoia and that there was nothing I could do that night to ease my concerns, I decided to put it to the back of my mind and hope for the best.

Come Wednesday, we would see.

Cum Wednesday I did see! I saw the light. I saw stars. I saw Jesus. I saw so many orgasms, I lost track. To be precise, I saw a perfectly sized cock, on my perfectly skilled lover, doing perfectly wonderful things, to my perfectly satisfied body. He even spanked. Hallelujah. Glory be! No doubt about it, he was my Magic Man.

That was only the beginning. Once our bodies touched, since our minds and spirits were already intertwined, we were on a rocket ride straight for the stars. I'd made the right choice. This was definitely the correct way to approach love.

That was two weeks ago!

Looking down at the sparkly diamond the Magic Man is offering me, I'm a seething mix of emotions. There's no question I'm madly in love and would be thrilled to spend my days with him by my side, but I'm still scared to death of the institution of marriage.

I've spent the last five years convinced I'd never wear one of those rings again. I love my butterfly life. I love my freedom. I love the sense of wide-open adventure I wake up with every day. I love being a creative bohemian. I'm a true Holly Golightly all the way from the top of my head to the tips of my pointy red heels. I have no desire to have a white picket fence and a common everyday existence. I don't want to be the little housewife a man comes home to after his days of grand adventure conquering the world. I don't ever want to be a taken for granted; to be a foregone conclusion. I love being desired and pursued. I love magic and mystery. I've had those diamonds before, and it meant a loss of the me I love. It's just not worth it. Even though I crave some form of security, adventure and freedom mean more to me than stability. All my recent decisions reflect that. I'm an artist. A dreamer. A free spirit.

In a matter of seconds, all of these contradictory thoughts and impulses rush through my head and flood me with terrible confusion.

"Love?"

Like a soul waking from a trance, I look up from the ring. The minute I see my Magic Man's eyes, all of my worries vanish. A wave of absolute joy flows over me and I start to cry with the beauty and rightness of the moment. A powerful revelation occurs to me. Despite my preconceived fears of marriage and commitment, this is not a man who wants to pin my butterfly wings to a board and turn me into a domesticated version of the wild heart I am. In fact, he is the very one who constantly admonishes me to do whatever it requires to keep my creative fires burning and produce the art that defines my existence. He loves my free-spirited ways. He would be horrified if I was anything less. He's a bold spirit; a visionary himself.

This is simply the man I love telling me that, in my madcap journeys fluttering around the garden of life, when I need a place to land and call home, I can make it with him. He is offering me the protection and shelter of a public commitment to reflect the private one we established that very first night at Home. He's willing to give me the set of roots I've always craved to go with the wings I fought so hard to have.

No doubt about it—when I let go of my baggage-induced perceptions of marriage, this feels right. In fact, it feels absolutely wonderful. I can have a partner to share my bohemian adventure with. Things shared are always better, good or bad. Hey, why didn't I think of this?

Without a second thought, a giant, "Yes!" bursts out of my lips. "Yes! Yes! Yes!" I yell, as he grabs me for a kiss. I start laughing. "Just so we are absolutely clear: I'm still going to spend a month or two alone writing in Paris at some point in my life."

"Oui, oui, Madame. I'll meet you there when you're done."

"And I can't cook, and have no intentions of learning."

"Lucky for you, I love cooking. I won't let you starve."

"I expect a lot."

"The great ones always do. So do I."

"I'm super emotional. It won't always be easy."

"Things worth having never are."

"I'll need my space."

"So will I."

"I still want to be pursued."

"I'll never tire of chasing you."

Pulling no punches, I say the most important thing, "You need to know that even when we're married, I won't stay if the relationship dies."

"Charity Gaye Finnestad, I love you for that! Don't worry, I'll never let our relationship die. You are the most amazing, interesting, warm, alive, and beautiful human being I've ever met. I love you. More than that, I respect you. I'm absolutely positive you will be a handful and challenge me on a daily basis. I'm up for the challenge." Tears of happiness start streaming down my face. He continues, "All those things about you that scared away the other guys—I love them! I love your honesty. I love your emotions. I love your big way of doing things. Those are the things that make you special. They define you. You need to understand—until I met you, I always felt alone. Since I've known you, I've never felt alone. That's irreplaceable, and I'll never let it die."

Pulling me closer, he give me a kiss hot enough to blast the Rockefeller tree into orbit. I melt into a puddle at his feet. "Anything else we need to cover, love?"

"No."

"Then can I put this baby on you?"

Looking down, I realize he's still holding the ring.

"Yes!" I scream again. A couple walking by pauses to see what the commotion is all about as he slides the ring on my finger. Brandishing my new bauble in the air and sporting a mega-watt grin, I yell, "He just gave me a diamond from the real *Breakfast at Tiffany's*, Tiffany's, of all places! I feel so Audrey Hepburn." They laugh, offering congratulations and best wishes as they continue on their way. Several more people stop and look at us. I'm bouncing with joy. Sensing my intentions, the Magic Man queries, "You're not about to do that Yippy Skippy thing, are you?"

"You bet I am!" I explode.

"Love, there are people…"

Before he can finish I'm pumping my arms up and down and slinging my legs out while the Magic Man, who I do believe is blushing, is scooting off to the side pretending he's never seen me before.

"Yippy skippy!" I whoop. Pointing at the Magic Man, "He finally found me!"

Everyone in Rockefeller Center turns as he dives around a corner, but not before I see the mega-watt smile covering my normally stoic new fiancé's face.

Watch out world, here we come—The Magic Man and Charity Gaye Finnestad—roots firmly planted, wings ready to fly.

VARIOUS FORMULAS:

Math formula…
$2 + 2 = 4$

Physics formula…
$E = mc^2$

Hollywood formula…
Blue balls = blackballed

POETRY IN MOTION

The Magic Man and I pop out of the car, and I toss the keys to the valet. My whole body is tingling with excitement. I give the Magic Man a cheeky grin and bust out a quick Yippy Skippy in the closed elevator as we head up to the reception desk. He laughs. Building security is going to get quite a giggle if they review the tapes from elevator number three and see the long-legged, high-heeled, crazy chick doing an Irish jig on crack. I don't care. I'm happy! This kind of joy requires a Yippy Skippy.

We're on our way to a meeting with a powerful figure in Tinsel Town, Golden. He loves my clog (blog+heels). That's the reason we're here. He wants to discuss the possibility of producing a TV version of *Hollywood in Heels*. It doesn't get cooler than that. Regardless of the outcome of this meeting, I feel like I've arrived. My writing is being acknowledged.

The Magic Man is attending to help me negotiate. He's good at that. He kicks ass and takes numbers on a daily basis for his real job, so being my sidekick is child's play to him.

We arrive at Golden's office, and he greets us with a giant hug. "I'm so happy to finally meet you."

He ushers us into a conference room and mentions that his head of production, a former agent from a powerful agency, will be joining us. He only uses the guy's first name, which is terribly common, but I get a strange premonition and say the last name out loud. Golden laughs and says, "You know him?"

Do I know him? Oh my god, do I know him!

When I was still brand-spanking new to this town, shortly after I met the German, she started dating Slick, an agent from a powerful agency. Slick was terribly charming, exceptionally funny, and incredibly likable. He was also barely half the German's height. She found him interesting for approximately five minutes, but not enough to sleep with him. Physically, he did nothing for her. He wasn't her type.

A couple of months after the German gave Slick his dating pink slip, we ran into him at a popular bar in town. He was with a large group of friends and invited us to join them at their table. Having nothing better to do, we said yes. The evening was magical. The German chatted with Slick's friends while he and I found ourselves holed up in a corner laughing for hours. I hadn't laughed that hard in a long time. No doubt about it, Slick was captivating.

When the Cinderella hour rolled around, I informed everyone, "It's time for me to say goodnight."

The German, who was not ready to go, decided to stay and bum a ride home from one of our friends at the bar. That was fairly typical. I turned into a pumpkin at midnight, and she was just getting started. As Slick gave me a good-bye hug, he asked for my number. "What can I say, I was with the wrong girl. You were always the one I wanted. I just met her first. Give me a chance, Charity. I really like you. We could have something."

I thought about it for a couple seconds and decided, what the heck. The German certainly wouldn't care. If she didn't sleep with a guy, she definitely didn't have feelings for him. She slept with guys she was only mildly interested in just for fun. On the other hand, I found him attractive. It wouldn't hurt to see where it went. I gave him my number.

The next morning, I was rudely awoken at seven-thirty by the insistent ringing of my phone. Picking up the annoying little noisemaker, I murmured a sleepy, "Hello."

"I fucked Slick, and it was horrible!" screamed the German.

Now I was awake!

"You what?"

"I know, I know. I didn't do it during the three weeks we dated, why do it now? Believe me, I'm asking myself the same question. He's a terrible fuck!"

The German wails into the phone as I try to pick my jaw up off the ground. That lecherous prick! What was with that whole spiel last night about how he really liked me? My god, does he use the same script on every woman?

"Wow, I didn't see that coming! I thought you didn't like him."

"I don't! I don't know what I was thinking. Now I'm totally grossed out."

"Oy vey."

It was one of those moments where I could go two ways. I could either tell my best friend about the phone number exchange and make her feel even worse about the whole situation, or I could pretend it never happened and leave her pride intact. Trust me, no woman who slept with a guy wants to hear that he told another woman she was his first choice just hours before. That would make you a sloppy second. There was no fucking way I was going to make my best friend feel like a sloppy second. On the other hand, if there was any chance of her hooking up again with him or falling for him, then I would have to tell her to warn her. But it was obvious from her reaction to the encounter that was out of the question, so I did the only thing that made sense. I kept my mouth shut.

About an hour after I got off the phone with the German my phone rang again. I didn't recognize the number, but answered anyway. Lo and behold, who should it be? Slick.

"Hey, Charity, I had such a great time with you last night. I'm so happy I ran into you again. Are you free for dinner tonight?"

"Are you serious?!" I asked, appalled.

"Of course, why wouldn't I be?"

"You fucked my best friend!" I shouted into the phone. This guy was unbelievable.

"You knew we dated. I didn't think you had a problem with that."

"Last night!"

Realization dawned on him, "Oh, she told you that? Well look, you always knew we dated. I didn't think her and I having a sexual history was a problem for you."

Was he for real?

"Sexual history, my ass! I happen to know she never slept with you when you dated, and that is the only reason I was willing to go out with you."

"Oh, she told you that, too? Look, we're all adults here," he said in that slow voice you use when speaking to a child. "Why don't we just pretend none of this happened?"

Slick spent the next ten minutes begging me not to tell the German about his advances. At some point, I let him off the hook and told him I saw no reason to. It would only hurt her. We would just move on with our own lives and pretend his bad behavior never happened.

Four weeks later, I was having dinner at Yamashiro with the German, her dashing lover Adonis (a famous German actor), and a pile of his movie friends. The German, terribly upset, showed me an endless string of text messages from Slick telling her how much he adored her, missed her, and really wanted to see her. She was literally wracked with guilt about not liking him. "Charity, he is such a nice guy. I feel like a complete jerk for blowing him off. He just doesn't do it for me. I don't know how to let him down gently. What do I say?"

It was too much. Watching my amazing, big-hearted friend steeped in guilt and angst over a lousy liar who used women like toilet paper made me furious. Before there hadn't been a reason to tell her, now there was.

"Okay," I said taking a deep breath. "I don't want to hear another word about poor, sweet Slick. There is nothing sweet about that slime ball."

I proceeded to give her the rundown on what had happened the night they hooked up, and his call to me the next day. She was furious. Who wouldn't be? Right there at the table, in front of her new lover and his friends, she picked up her cell phone and gave Slick a well-earned piece of her mind. She finished by yelling, "Lose my number, asshole!" I thought she did great. He certainly had it coming.

When she got off the phone, I assumed the drama was over.

I couldn't be so lucky.

One week later, as the German sat on a flight back to her homeland for a vacation, I received a phone call. Once again, not recognizing the number I answered. Big mistake! It was Slick. He had waited until he knew the German had left town for his final assault. Both barrels blazing, he began a twenty-minute attack on my character. He screamed. He called me names. He told me I was a worthless excuse for a human being. A snake. A backstabber. A bitch. Those are the nice things he said. I refuse to even repeat the foul ones. He, in his lofty position of power, promised that he would make sure I never made it in this town. I was going to pay for my impudence. According to him, I was blackballed. I sat on the other end of the phone shaking like a leaf, too shocked to even hang up.

When his attack finally came to an end and he slammed down the phone, I burst into tears. I didn't realize I was still clutching the phone in shock until it started making the "disconnect" drone. Of course, all I wanted to do was to call the German and feel the comfort of her support, but Slick had made sure I wouldn't even have that. Instead, I spent the whole night sleepless, terrified that he was going to break into my place and beat me up. It was weeks before I quit feeling on edge.

That was five years ago.

Standing in Golden's office I mentally check back in and answer his question, "Yes, as a matter of fact I do know Slick." (beat) "He dated my best friend a couple of years ago."

Golden shakes his head and grins, "What a small world."

"That it is!"

Glancing at the Magic Man, I realize he's put Slick's name and the story together. I give him the "I've got this covered" look. He nods.

At that exact moment, the door flies open and in walks Slick, a cheesy smile smeared across his face. He's in full schmooze mode. First he sees the Magic Man and extends his hand. He knows what my husband does for a living and wants to be on his good side. Mid-shake, he notices little old me standing slightly behind my Magic Man. Like a deer in headlights, Slick freezes. His face goes white. Golden, clueless to the underlying dynamics, teases his friend, "Charity told us everything, man."

I didn't think it was possible, but with that, Slick goes even whiter. Beads of sweat break out on his forehead as he warily studies me. I can see his brain spinning. He knows his boss wants to work with me. He knows I have every reason to hate him. He now believes I told his boss and the Magic Man everything. He has no clue what to do to get himself out of this situation. It is fully in my power to torture him. The tables are turned. I'm in control. I can do whatever I want. What will I do?

The only thing I can.

"I told him you dated the German."

I extend the olive branch and my hand. "It's a pleasure to see you again, Slick."

The fear drains out of his body. In the blink of an eye, he transforms back into his charming public persona. If I hadn't seen it myself, I almost wouldn't believe what just took place. Like seeing the corpse underneath the living, breathing man.

In full schmooze mode, he pumps my hand and addresses the men, "Isn't this girl great? I've always loved her! Do you know we go way back?"

And with that, he begins a full-court press to get the rights to produce my show.

As I participate in the discussion about what making the show will entail, and what role I want to play in its production, half of my mind is marveling at the way life works.

You know that famous saying, "Revenge is a dish best served cold?" I think it is dead wrong. Forget about revenge. When someone does you wrong, there is only one thing you can gracefully do: let go, and move on.

The truth is revenge is a dish best not served at all. Instead, live your best life, and trust the glorious universe in all its infinite wisdom to serve you up a generous helping of the best dish around: poetic justice. I can assure you, it's much tastier and far more rewarding.

Spotlight-itis [spät-**līt**-ī-təs]
noun

1. A pathological addiction to basking in the glow of attention from other humans.
2. A compulsive need to be in the spotlight.
3. The misguided belief that nothing you do in private counts.

Example: "Her spotlight-itis was so out of control that she failed to recognize the difference between healthy and toxic shades of limelight."

BE THE BULB

Well, how do you like that? I gaze at fifty million black stretch limos lined up like dominos to pick up fifty million rock stars, music industry execs, and high heel-sporting chicks like myself. Oh geez, just what I need.

The Magic Man and I are attempting to leave the 50th Annual Grammy Awards After Party thrown by Universal—"attempting," being the operative word. I'm so tired I can barely see straight, and figuring out which limo is ours is going to be like finding a needle in a haystack. Technically, I should be attending five more record label after parties with the Magic Man and his boss, Full Throttle, but tonight I'm physically incapable of doing my part to maintain the "model" part of the "Party Like a Model/Rock Star."

"You're letting the home team down," Full Throttle razzed me when I attempted to bid him and the rest of our party crew farewell. "We're just getting started."

"What can I say. I'm not your average anorexic, food-phobic model. I require fuel," I replied.

In true Full Throttle fashion, he handed me another drink.

"Not the liquid kind," I laughed, "I need a nosh."

Being a gentleman, Full Throttle sent a cocktail waiter to scrounge up something for me to eat. When the forager came back defeated, Full

Throttle gave Magic Man and I leave to go. We immediately exited before I fainted from hunger.

So here we stand on the curb, missing out on the party, searching for our wheels, thanks to my super-light-speed metabolism. Yes, it's true; I need a healthy dose of nutrition every few hours, or I'm a wreck. I've finally come to accept the fact that this is my Achilles' heel. Since the limo picked us up at three o'clock, and it is now going on eleven without a single bite passing my lips, I'm practically a walking zombie. At this point, my only hope of resuscitation is an In-N-Out burger and a good night's sleep.

Wow, though, what a night! Despite my exhausted state, I wouldn't have missed it for anything. I got to see one of my all-time favorites, Tina Turner, tearing up the stage, looking like a schoolgirl at sixty-eight in silver spandex. And I had an epic realization: Sometimes in life you are lucky enough to get publicly rewarded for your hard work, but even if you are not, you are still a winner if the work itself is your reward.

In a capitalistic, success-driven culture, this is not an easy concept to grasp. Our society is entirely outcome-based. I struggle with this constantly. Many times I get so caught up in the end-goal of recognition, respect, and a paycheck that I forget to experience the actual joy of creation. A couple of months ago, I was talking with the Professor and he was absolutely horrified about something that had happened that day. It appeared that a European art exhibition he was being featured in had billed him as an Internationally Renowned Artist and put his name in LARGE PRINT compared to the other artists being shown. He was appalled and mortified. Never mind that the Professor is an Internationally Renowned Artist, deserving of all the acclaim he receives—he was having none of it. He called the people in charge and insisted that they remove the title and put his name in small print like everyone else.

I found the whole thing utterly hysterical. It so clearly reflected the discrepancy in where we were in our careers. I would have loved to have a billboard that called me an Internationally Renowned Author. As to the size of my name… "Could you please make it larger? I don't think they can see it from space."

I shared my thoughts with the Professor, and he shrugged his humble shoulders at my egotistical ramblings. "Just do what you love, Charity. And do it well."

Tonight, as I sat in total shock watching Kanye West's arrogant attitude about his award, I started to understand what the Professor was talking about. I mean, Kanye actually had the audacity to say, "I deserve this." Discrediting all the work and creations of the other contenders. Who's to say if he did? But there was something terribly tragic about the feeling one got that he performs for the outcome (money, recognition, women, etc.), and not for the love of creation. One wonders that, if all those perks weren't possible, would he would still spend his days rapping away for the pure love of rhyme? I seriously doubt it. I found myself completely turned off. It was even more sharply contrasted when Vince Gill stood up and humbly accepted his award, ending with the poetic statement, "In the democracy of music, every note is equal." I'm pretty sure if he were a total unknown with no hope of a paycheck, he would still be strumming his heart out every day for pure love of melody.

Sitting in my seat, listening to those vastly differing acceptance speeches, I had my lightbulb moment. It was really simple: Things created with love and dedication to the creation, not the outcome, possess a kind of magic and beauty that outcome-based creations do not. Whether you are digging a ditch or working on a masterpiece novel, it has to be done for you alone, not for someone else. It's not about seeing your name in lights. It's about shining your light into everything you do. If that is the way you approach life, you will always be rewarded with a sense of satisfaction and happiness. Any public rewards will just be icing on the cake.

My god, that's the answer to the quest I've been on ever since I drove that bloody U-Haul into town five years ago. I came to this city searching for the wrong things! I honestly believed I needed an external map to happiness—sketched out by someone else and given to me to follow. Fuck, that's how I'd lived my life to that point. I danced like a marionette for my parents, the church, my schools, and then my ex-husbands. I let other people's approval be my reason for being. I didn't know any other way. That's why, when I came to LA, I wanted a tastemaker to "discover" my "it-ness." I hadn't found myself, so I thought someone else could help me do it. They would give me my creative direction, recognize my writing's value, and hand me a clear life purpose. I thought a spotlight shined on my life by someone else was required for it to have meaning. I was Kanye.

I was completely wrong!

The value was in the journey itself—not the targeted destination or the external approval. My making that crazy pilgrimage and leaving everything I knew behind put me in a position that forced growth. It was do or die. As a result, my writing grew, my wealth of experiences grew, and my understanding of who I was grew. Everything that wasn't really me fell by the wayside. I couldn't afford to carry it and survive. The things that remained were the real me: my true passions. Blazing my own trail with no outside voices telling me how to do it or where to go, I discovered my own internal compass; my true north.

I'm a writer, a storyteller.

Just like the ancient oracles who wove their magic around fire pits, putting life's experiences in context and illustrating the adventure of being human, I need to tell stories. I need to see the meaning behind things. I need things to possess clear beginnings, middles, and ends. I need arcs, moments of realization, plot points. I need to use words to paint pictures and communicate. It's how I make sense of the world. It doesn't matter how hard it is at times. It doesn't matter if I ever make money doing it. It doesn't matter if I expose myself to ridicule for my ideas. It doesn't matter if people love or hate me. I live for it. It lives in me.

Let's face it; I've been writing since the day I could hold a pen, and I'll be writing until they scatter my ashes in the wind, whether anyone else reads my words or not. Of course, I'd love to have tons of readers all over the world. Who wouldn't? But whatever happens with my writing—whether I produce a TV show or don't, whether I'm published or not, whether people hang onto my every word or mock my every effort—I will not stop putting my thoughts, dreams, stories, and ideas down on paper. The act of writing itself is my salvation, my purpose, my constant. The Professor was right. Doing what you love is the reward.

"Baby, it's over here."

I'm yanked out of my earth-shattering epiphany by my own personal hero—the Magic Man.

Who needs a knight on a white horse when you have a man in blue jeans and a black sports coat who can spot your wheels out of a million look-alikes? Teetering on my four-inch stilettos toward my magic carpet ride home, with no spotlight guiding my way or flashes of paparazzi following my every move, I decide on my new life slogan, the creed that will guide my steps from here on out…

"Screw external illumination. Just be the Bulb!"

ACKNOWLEDGMENTS

Every person who enters your life and plays a significant part forms your character, even when their role is to create resistance and challenge you. With that in mind, I want to thank all the people who have helped make me who I am today. My mom, Betty Finnestad, who embodies generosity and optimism. My father, Chris Finnestad, who taught me to dream by example. My sister, Melody Joy, who graced my life with laughter, and whose passing made me realize the value and permanence of love. Rachel Dawn Grimes, who's had my back literally and figuratively since the days when I sported a shiny, silver brace-face. Peter Jay, who generously shared his family with me. Suzanne Bowers, who never gives up on those she loves. Heidi Hagen, whose warmth and grace helped keep my heart from turning to ice in Oregon. Penny Gerbode, who prevented a starving writer from actually starving for an entire year. Tommy Lamey, the best landlord, surrogate uncle, and tuna fish sandwich-maker a girl could ever hope to find. Peter Katsis, a dear friend, and my favorite soup kitchen. Christian Moeller, who you can always count on to say it straight. Jesse Stagg, the warmest bear hug in all of greater LA. Roxana Lima, who keeps my life in order and helps take care of my Prince while I write. My Prince, Talbot Kondrk, who loans his Mama to a computer screen for several hours a day so that she can tell her stories.

Then there is the posse; my chosen sisterhood. I never would have survived my Homerian-like Odyssey in Tinsel Town without them, so here's to the posse. Annique Delphine, photographer extraordinaire, who's cut from the same cloth and has made my life better since the moment she pranced into it on her ridiculously long legs. Eliza Bane, the pink-feathered pal who loves my poetry and elevated my confidence during a very tough time. Dr. Nicole Meise, the "smart ass" I can always count on. The Duchess, who ultimately broke my heart, but who deeply enriched my life for a season. Simone Bargetze, who lives boldly on the edge. Simone Ott Caduff, who dances like no one is watching. Michael Crook, who never does anything half way. Viviana Suaya, my big sister champion. Brook Yakin, my Wicked friend, whose razor wit can make me laugh through tears. Sara Melson, my favorite mother earth goddess. Sarah Imparato, whose boundless enthusiasm is contagious. Alexandra Grant, who challenges me to dream big and always lifts my spirits. Blanda Eggenschwiller, my little sister with the old soul. Heather Collins, who still believes in fairies and magic. Christina Van Der Schaar, my Swiss treasure. Manda Ersgard, my Swedish soul sister.

And then there are the men. I won't name them, but they know who they are. Thank you for the laugher and the tears, the love and the hate, the spankings and the tickles, the orgasms and the affection, the heartbreak and the heart expansion. I feel deeply grateful for your presence in my life, even though it may not have worked out as either of us hoped. I hope you are enjoying your journey as much as I am, and I hope you find the things that you are looking for along the way. Big kiss and a little bite.

Thanks to Emily Florence, whose patience, cheerleading, and overall encouragement have helped make this book what it is today. Thanks to Elizabeth D'Errico for graciously helping me mind my Ps and Qs. Thanks to Kevin Yorn and Alex Kohner, the best lawyers a girl could ask for. Thanks to Ted Gerdes for helping me protect my "ass-ettes." Thanks to Bruce Harris for helping me turn this into a physical reality.

Thanks to Jenn McCartney at Skyhorse Publishing for her commitment and enthusiasm.

Thanks to all my lovely friends who let me use their gorgeous mugs in my book: Blanda Eggenschwiller, Ania Spiering, Nicole Meise, Nina Smidt, Maia Smidt, Carla Houston, Jennifer Whyte, Tamara Edwards, Catherine Townsend, Serge Hoeltschi, Joseph James Hayes, Michael Crook, Sara Melson, Jesse Stagg, Ed Rackham, and Annique Delphine. Thanks to Bethany McCarty for doing great makeup for the loft shoot, and Joseph James Hayes for amazing hairstyling. Thanks to Adolfo Suaya and Joseph for letting me shoot in their spaces.

Last but not least, I'd like to thank the two men who really made this happen. First, the gallant Peter Lehner, my favorite tirader, who convinced me to write the blog *Hollywood in Heels* and believed in me from the moment we met. The value of belief by another individual cannot be overstated. It's the tiebreaker that tips the scale in your favor in the battle between your demons and your angels on hard cold nights of self-doubt. It's a lifeline. It's rocket fuel. It's invaluable. And for this, I will always owe one of the most interesting and intelligent men I have ever had the privilege of knowing: Peter Lehner.

And finally, I'd like to thank my husband, my Magic Man, Robert Kondrk. From the moment we met, I knew that I'd met my match, or as my mom says, "Finally, a man who can keep up with you." We're nothing alike on the outside. A more opposite personality doesn't exist. I'm gregarious. He's stoic. I'm intuitive. He's pragmatic. I laugh so hard I sometimes snort. He says, "That's funny." But on the inside, where the important things live—one's dreams, beliefs, codes of honor, and passions—we're cut from the same cloth. We posses the same worldview, the same spiritual view, and a mad appreciation for each other's intelligence. From this place of mutual respect and attraction, Robert has steadily, quietly, and determinedly championed my creativity from day one. Every time I met an obstacle developing Hollywood in Heels *into a show and wanted to throw in the towel, he talked me into going another round. He convinced me the blog ought to be a book, and that the book deserved to have its day in the sun.*

So here it is, out of the dark recesses of my mind and onto this page in front of you. Without all the aforementioned people and their contribution, this wouldn't exist; and without you, it wouldn't have its moment in the sun.

So my final thanks is to you, my reader, for sitting down with me around the metaphorical campfire and sharing my story. May you also find happiness in the journey, and may you always realize the value of your own inner light. Let's be the bulb together, and all make this world a brighter place.

Big kiss,
Charity